YOUNG MATHEMATICIANS
AT WORK

YOUNG MATHEMATICIANS AT WORK

CONSTRUCTING NUMBER SENSE, ADDITION, AND SUBTRACTION

CATHERINE TWOMEY FOSNOT
MAARTEN DOLK

HEINEMANN • Portsmouth, NH

Heinemann

361 Hanover Street
Portsmouth, NH, 03801-3912
www.heinemann.com

Offices and agents throughout the world

Table 7.1 is reprinted with permission from "The Harmful Effects of Algorithms in Grades 1–4" by Constance Kamii and Ann Dominick in *The Teaching and Learning of Algorithms in School Mathematics* by the National Council of Teachers of Mathematics.

The photo of the tapestry "L'artithmetique" is used courtesy of the Musée national du Moyen Age, Paris, Thermas at hotel de Cluny.

This material is supported in part by the National Science Foundation under Grant No. 9550080 and Grant No. 9911841. Any opinions, findings, and conclusions or recommendations expressed in this material are those of the authors and do not necessarily reflect the views of the National Science Foundation.

Library of Congress Cataloging-in-Publication Data

Fosnot, Catherine Twomey.
  Young mathematicians at work : constructing number sense, addition, and subtraction /
Catherine Twomey Fosnot, Maarten Dolk.
    p. cm.
  Includes bibliographical references and index.
  ISBN 0-325-00353-X (alk. paper)
  1. Mathematics—Study and teaching (Elementary) I. Dolk, Maarten Ludovicus
Antonius Marie, 1952– II. Title.

QA135.5 .F6318 2001
372.7—dc21

                                                          2001016587

Editors: Victoria Merecki and Leigh Peake
Cover design: Darci Mehall/Aureo Design
Cover photograph: Haynes Images
Text photographs: Herbert Seignoret
Manufacturing: Louise Richardson

Printed in the United States of America on acid-free paper

      13 14 RRD   19

To the teachers with whom we have worked
and from whom we have learned so much,
particularly Karen During,
who died of leukemia in the third year of the project

CONTENTS

CHAPTER THREE: NUMBER SENSE ON THE HORIZON

CHAPTER FOUR: PLACE VALUE ON THE HORIZON

CHAPTER FIVE: DEVELOPING MATHEMATICAL MODELS

CHAPTER SIX: ADDITION AND SUBTRACTION FACTS ON THE HORIZON

CHAPTER SEVEN: ALGORITHMS VERSUS NUMBER SENSE

CHAPTER EIGHT: DEVELOPING EFFICIENT COMPUTATION WITH MINILESSONS

ACKNOWLEDGMENTS

The two names on the cover of this book mean only that we are the ones who finally sat down at the keyboard. The ideas included here grew out of a collaboration between researchers at the Freudenthal Institute and the faculty and staff of Mathematics in the City, a professional development program sponsored by the City College of New York. Together, we worked, reflected, talked, and experimented.

First and foremost, we thank our colleague Willem Uittenbogaard, whose voice is evident on every page. He has been an integral force in developing the project, designing and structuring the activities we use, and participating in our classroom investigations. He left the Netherlands and spent two years living and working in New York City, coteaching the institutes and follow-up courses and supporting teachers in their classrooms as they reformed their practice. We all grew to love him and respect his knowledge of mathematics, his understanding of the Freudenthal Institute's work, and his sensitivity to the cultures that are a part of New York City. The mini-lessons built around problem strings (see Chapter 8) are largely the result of the work he did with us. He worked tirelessly to make the program a success, and we are extremely grateful for his professionalism, his generosity, and his dedication.

Staff members Sherrin Hersch, Betina Zolkower, Emily Dann, and Judit Kerekes all made invaluable contributions. In addition to teaching, Sherrin was the co–principal investigator on the project, registering some 450 teachers in various and sundry courses, dealing with the paperwork, and acting as our liaison with the schools. This was often thankless, time-consuming work, and we want to acknowledge the hours she gave to it, as well as the gift of her calmness and sanity. We are especially grateful for Betina's energy and her intellect, for the way she challenged us to avoid trivialized word problems, pushing us instead to make the contexts rich and challenging. She was the advisor for many of the projects teachers tried in their classrooms and is primarily responsible for the richness of some of the investigations described in this book. (Susannah Blum's Seed Time investigation, in Chapter 4, and Toni Cameron and Diane Jackson's project on routines, in Chapter 3, are but two examples.) We thank Emily for the depth of mathematical knowledge she contributed and for commuting from Rutgers so tirelessly, always lending a supportive ear to our teachers and helping them in any way she could. We thank Judit for the many hours she donated without pay because she believed in the project.

The project's smooth operation we owe to Herbert Seignoret. Hired initially as a part-time graduate assistant, he soon began working full time, videotaping in classrooms, helping with budgets, payroll, data collection, and general office management. We all grew to rely on him and his amazing ability to do twenty things at once—and well.

We are especially grateful to the teachers and children whose voices fill these pages. The book exists because of them and the things they tried in their classrooms.

Many other colleagues read portions of the manuscript and provided helpful comments. In the spring of 2000, Cathy spent her sabbatical at the Freudenthal Institute in order to complete the manuscript. While there, she shared an office with Koeno Gravemeijer. He not only read and commented on various portions of the manuscript, he also challenged us with his writing on models and in many ways brought the book to a higher level. Other colleagues from the Netherlands also read and commented on various portions of the manuscript: Ed de Moor, Frans van Galen, Jean Marie Kraemer, Anne Coos Vuurmans, and Arthur Bakker. Conversations with them helped us formulate the way we describe number relations. In particular, we want to thank Marja van den Heuvel-Panhuizen from the Freudenthal Institute, who helped us design our approach to assessment and whose work is described throughout Chapter 9. Funding for the project came from the National Science Foundation and the Exxon Educational Foundation. We are extremely grateful for their support.

Last, we thank our editors at Heinemann, Leigh Peake, Victoria Merecki, and Alan Huisman, for their belief in the project and their insightful suggestions for tightening the manuscript.

PREFACE

This book is a culmination of a long and fruitful journey characterized by collaboration, experimentation, reflection, and growth. More than ten years ago we learned of each other's work with teachers in our respective countries —Cathy in the United States, Maarten in the Netherlands. Both of us cared deeply about helping mathematics teachers base their practice on how people learn mathematics, how they come to see the world through a mathematical lens—how they come to *mathematize* their world. Both of us had done research on teachers' beliefs, their visions of practice, and how these beliefs affected their decisions, and we were attempting to develop inservice programs that would enable teachers to reform their practice.

Cathy had previously been involved with the SummerMath for Teachers program at Mount Holyoke College, coteaching the summer institutes and working alongside elementary teachers in their classrooms. She had also developed and directed the Center for Constructivist Teaching, a graduate preservice program at Connecticut State University. Whether she was teaching children mathematics or helping teachers learn to teach mathematics, the learning psychology commonly known as constructivism was at the core of her work.

Maarten, a researcher and developer at the Freudenthal Institute in the Netherlands, had been involved in the development of inservice materials and multimedia learning environments for teachers. He also had directed the PANAMA inservice project in the Netherlands, and had been involved in the implementation of the Realistic Mathematics curricula, for which the Freudenthal Institute is now so widely known. Whether he was thinking about teaching children mathematics or helping teachers learn to teach mathematics, the didactic now commonly known as realistic mathematics was at the core of his work.

In the United States, much reform was already under way, aligned with the new principles and standards published by the National Council of Teachers of Mathematics. Much attention was being paid to how students learn mathematics and to what the constructivist theory of learning might mean for teaching. Teachers were encouraged to become facilitators and questioners instead of transmitters, to use manipulatives, and to foster collaborative learning and discussion in order to support learners' constructions. Although teachers began to have a good idea about how their role needed to shift, they were given little assistance in determining content and little direction regarding what problems or investigations to pursue over time.

The focus in the United States was on learners' strategies and the big ideas surrounding them. And this was important. But the sequence of activities in the curricula being developed, even when supposedly aligned with the reform, was often based on the *discipline* of mathematics. For example, fractions were taught by way of simple part-to-whole shading activities in the lower grades, then in the higher grades as ratios, as partitioning, and finally as operators. Learners' methods of developing ideas and strategies were usually discussed in relation to pedagogy (principles of learning and teacher behavior that supports learning), if at all. Constructivist-based professional development helped teachers see the big ideas their learners were struggling with, but little attention was paid to *didactics*—a scientific theory of instruction relating to developing, stretching, and supporting mathematical learning over time. (In fact, the word *didactics* often has a negative connotation in the United States, one associated with self-correcting materials and direct instruction, not with development.)

In Europe the term *didactics* has a very different meaning. The French, for example, speak of *situation didactique,* meaning problems or situations that will enable learners to grow mathematically. The Dutch structure problem contexts in order to challenge and support learners developmentally. They spend years researching the effect of a sequence of carefully crafted problems. So, too, in Japan. Together, educators mold and craft problems in ways that strengthen their power to develop mathematical thinking. Teachers try these problems and then discuss which ones worked, which ones didn't, how they might be changed, what should come next.

The didactic in the Netherlands was based primarily on the work of the renowned mathematician Hans Freudenthal. As early as the sixties, Freudenthal had argued that people learn mathematics by actively investigating realistic problems. He claimed that mathematics was actually an activity of "mathematizing" the world, of modeling, of schematizing, of structuring one's world mathematically. Working with Dutch educators for over twenty years prior to his death in 1990, he was instrumental in reforming Dutch mathematics teaching based on "realistic mathematics." Within this framework, researchers formulated "learning lines" by studying the development of mathematical ideas historically, as well as the developmental progression of children's strategies and ideas about various mathematical topics. Then they crafted a series of contexts they thought might support children's natural development, often molding problems to facilitate disequilibrium or to bring insights to the fore. Finally they tested these problems with children, revised them as necessary, and prepared them as curricula. Less attention was given to pedagogy or to cognitive construction. While children were understood to move at their own pace developmentally, the class was taught as a whole. There was little attempt to support individual investigation or inquiry or to look at the belief systems of teachers regarding learning.

The American and Dutch educators both held an important piece of the puzzle. The Americans were thinking deeply about learning; how learners needed to engage in cognitive reordering; the importance of disequilibrium, reflection, and discussion; and the importance of big ideas. Teachers were analyzing their beliefs about learning and about their pedagogy. Classrooms were taking on the flavor of active workshops. But the Americans didn't know how to support development over time, how to use context as a didactic. The Dutch did.

In the late eighties we began to collaborate seriously. Cathy brought groups of teachers from Connecticut to the Netherlands for one-week intensive workshops, organized by Maarten and his colleague Willem Uittenbogaard. Maarten and other colleagues from the Freudenthal Institute (Jan De Lange, Frans van Galen) came to Connecticut State University. In 1993, Cathy left Connecticut State University and took a position at the City College of the City University of New York. We began to design a large-scale inservice program that would involve five school districts in New York City over five years, a project known as Mathematics in the City. The project was funded by the National Science Foundation and the Exxon Educational Foundation and began in 1995.

During the next five years we worked with over 450 elementary teachers in New York City and developed several demonstration sites. Our inservice program began with a two-week intensive institute focused on teaching and learning. In this beginning institute, we attempted to deepen teachers' knowledge of the mathematics they teach and to help them see themselves as mathematicians willing to raise questions, puzzle, and mathematize. Staff members then joined teachers in their classrooms for a year, coteaching with them as they attempted to reform their mathematics teaching. At the same time, participants took a course focused on children's strategies, the big ideas they grapple with, and the models they develop as they attempt to mathematize their world.

Throughout the project, we interviewed teachers, analyzed children's work, and videotaped lessons; together we constructed what we came to call a "landscape of learning." Classroom teachers continued to receive support as they collaborated with colleagues, and several went on to do field research and adjunct teaching with the program.

While our inservice project was successful, this book is not about the program per se. Throughout our five-year collaboration, we formulated new beliefs about learning and teaching mathematics. We challenged each other to go beyond our beginnings—to take our strengths to the table but to stay open and learn from each other. Together with our staff and our teachers, we entered new frontiers. This book offers stories from our classrooms and describes the ways we approach teaching and the contexts we use to promote investigations and inquiry. It describes the landscape over which our young students journeyed as they constructed ideas about number, addition, and subtraction.

This book is a culmination, then, but it is also a beginning, the first in a series of books and inservice materials (prekindergarten through grade 8) on the number strand. The second book in the series will focus on multiplication and division in grades 3 through 5. The third will focus on fractions, decimals, and percents in grades 5 through 8. Related inservice materials will include CD-ROMs and videotapes with accompanying manuals. Our beliefs about teaching and learning mathematics will be woven throughout.

ABOUT THIS BOOK

Chapter 1 describes and illustrates our beliefs about what it means to do and learn mathematics. We discuss it as *mathematizing,* but we ground it in the progression of strategies, the development of big ideas, and the emergence of modeling because we hold a constructivist view of learning.

Chapter 2 explains what we mean by the "landscape of learning." For teachers to open up their teaching, they need to have a deep understanding of this landscape, of the strategies, big ideas, and models children construct, of the landmarks they pass as they journey towards numeracy. This chapter also contrasts "word problems" with true problematic situations that support and enhance investigation and inquiry.

Chapter 3 takes us back to the preschool classroom to see the early part of the journey—young children beginning to construct number sense and teachers facilitating this journey by way of games, contexts, routines, and investigations.

Chapter 4 is a close-up of the horizon of place value. Exploring the development of number systems in various cultures and across time, we see that young children construct their knowledge of our number system in just this way. Several classroom investigations illustrate ways to engage and support children as they construct this huge idea—an idea that took mathematicians centuries to develop.

It is impossible to talk about mathematizing without talking about modeling. Chapter 5 defines what we mean by modeling and gives examples of how learners construct models as they try to make sense of their world mathematically. In this chapter we also describe the importance of context in developing children's ability to model and show how teachers can help children make the leap from *models of situations* to *models as tools for thinking.*

Chapters 6, 7, and 8 focus on addition and subtraction. We discuss how to go about teaching the basic facts. We describe the *rekenrek,* a Dutch manipulative that supports the development of children's addition and subtraction strategies, illustrating how to make and use it and showing children working with it. We discuss what it means to calculate using number sense and whether or not algorithms should still be the goal of computation instruction. Although we conclude that children must be allowed to construct their own strategies, we offer many minilessons that will help children develop what we call a repertoire of strategies based on a deep understanding of number relationships and operations. We argue for the construction of a sense of "number space" comprising friendly numbers, neighbors, and leaps. We present examples of teachers using strings of related problems and the open number line to develop this sense of "number space."

In Chapter 9 we address how one assesses "mathematizing." We describe performance and portfolio assessment, but we show how they can be strengthened by making the "mathematizing" more visible and by using the landscape of learning as a tool. We argue that assessment should inform teaching.

Last, in Chapter 10, we focus on the teacher as learner. How do we help teachers begin to see themselves as mathematicians, be willing to inquire, work at their mathematical edge, appreciate puzzlement? We open a window into an inservice classroom and invite you to mathematize along with the teachers we describe.

Like all human beings, mathematicians find ways to make sense of their reality. They set up relationships, they quantify them, and they prove them to others. For teachers to engage children in this process, they must understand and appreciate the nature of mathematics. They must be willing to investigate and inquire—and to derive enjoyment from doing so. The book you hold is primarily about that—how teachers and children come to see their own lived worlds mathematically, their journeys as they pursue the hard work of constructing big ideas, strategies, and mathematical models in the collaborative community of the classroom.

YOUNG MATHEMATICIANS
AT WORK

15 16 17 18 19 20 21 22 23 24
Wednesday
Morning Meeting
Silent Reading
Read Aloud
Snack
Math
Number of beads
12 1 2
13 1 3
14 1 4
15 1
16 1
17 1
18 1

1 | "MATHEMATICS" OR "MATHEMATIZING"?

The United States suffers from "innumeracy" in its general population, "math avoidance" among high school students, and 50 percent failure among college calculus students. Causes include starvation budgets in the schools, mental attrition by television, parents [and teachers] who don't like math. There's another, unrecognized cause of failure: misconception of the nature of mathematics. . . . It's the questions that drive mathematics. Solving problems and making up new ones is the essence of mathematical life. If mathematics is conceived apart from mathematical life, of course it seems—dead.

—*Reuben Hersh*, What Is Mathematics, Really?

A mathematician, like a painter or a poet, is a maker of patterns. . . . The mathematician's patterns, like the painter's or the poet's, must be beautiful. . . . There is no permanent place in the world for ugly mathematics.

—*Godfrey H. Hardy*, A Mathematician's Apology

It is a truism that the purpose of teaching is to help students learn. Yet in the past teaching and learning were most often seen as two separate, even polar, processes. Teaching was what teachers did. They were supposed to know their subject matter and be able to explain it well. Students were supposed to do the learning. They were expected to work hard, practice, and listen to understand. If they didn't learn, it was their fault; they had a learning disability, they needed remediation, they were preoccupied, they were lazy. Even when we spoke of development, it was usually to assess learners to see whether they were developmentally ready for the teacher's instruction.

Interestingly, in some languages, *learning* and *teaching* are the same word. In Dutch, for example, the distinction between learning and teaching is made only by the preposition. The verb is the same. *Leren aan* means teaching; *leren van* means learning. When learning and teaching are so closely related, they will be integrated in learning/teaching frameworks: teaching will be seen as closely related to learning, not only in language and thought but also in action. If learning doesn't happen, there has been no teaching. The actions of learning and teaching are inseparable.

Of course, different teachers have different styles for helping children

1

learn. But behind these styles are frameworks based on teachers' beliefs about the learning/teaching process. These frameworks, in turn, affect how teachers interact with children, what questions they ask, what ideas they pursue, even what activities they design or select. Teachers make many important decisions—some of them in a split second in the nitty-gritty of the classroom. In making these decisions, some teachers are led by the structure of mathematics or the textbook series, others by the development of the children.

LEARNING AND TEACHING IN THE CLASSROOM

Join us in Madeline Chang's K–1 classroom in New York City, and let's try to determine what learning/teaching framework underlies her decision making.

"Hey . . . I see a pattern!" exclaims Roland, excitedly. He is referring to a big chart depicting combinations of dimes and pennies; his classmates are all nestled around him on the meeting rug.

Earlier Madeline had told the twenty-seven students in her class about her grandmother in China, who made beautiful glass bead necklaces. For several weeks the children have been making similar necklaces using five beads of one color, then five of another, then repeating five of the first color, five of the second, and so on. They have made a lot of different sizes, some small enough to be bracelets. They plan the necklaces first by making drawings or using Unifix cubes, since the beads are tiny, made of glass, and expensive. The necklaces will be sold at a PTA meeting for a penny a bead. Today the students are calculating how much each piece of jewelry will cost and making big charts of the combinations of dimes and pennies customers can use to pay for them.

"See," Roland continues excitedly, "there is a two over there [*he points to the numeral 2 under the picture of a dime*] and a zero there [*he points to the 0 under the picture of the penny*], and those are the same numbers in the twenty! And it's the same with the fourteen. It's a one [*dime*] and a four [*pennies*]!"

"Oh wow, Roland, that's interesting," Madeline says with pleasure. She has designed this investigation with just this "horizon" of place value in mind. She hoped that by suggesting the students charge a dime for ten beads and by having them make charts listing the resulting costs, the patterns Roland is now noticing would become the focus of a discussion. To enhance this important mathematical teaching moment, she attempts to pull other children into the conversation. "Who understands what Roland is noticing?"

"I do," says Tara, jumping up to join Roland at the chart. "See, 1 and 4, that's 14, and 2 and 0, that's 20."

Madeline tries to heighten the mathematical teaching moment by creating a little puzzlement. "But one and four added together don't make fourteen. How much do they make?" She succeeds.

"Five," Tara responds with a perplexed expression.

"Yes," Madeline acknowledges. "So why would the chart have this pattern, I wonder?" She looks around at the many intent, puzzled faces.

"Oh . . . I think I know." Ellie ventures a tentative explanation. "It's ten cents, so it goes up to four. . . ."

"Goes up to four?" Madeline repeats.

Ellie explains, this time with a little more conviction. "One dime equals ten cents, so it goes up to fourteen, not five."

Stephen joins the conversation. "I know what she means. If you move the 0 over to the 1, it makes the 10. It looks like ten, but it isn't."

"No, it is," Ellie shakes her head in disagreement, "because it's not one penny, it's one dime. It looks like just one cent, but it is under the dime and one dime equals ten cents."

This idea, that ten things (in a group) can also be one group, is such a big idea for these children! They have only recently figured out how to count meaningfully, attributing only one counting word to each object, and now this original counting strategy seems contradicted! It is not one word for one object, but one word for a group of ten! How can ten simultaneously be one?

Ellie's argument begins to convince several of the other children, so Madeline extends the discussion. "What about where the numeral two is by twenty cents?"

"That's two dimes!" several children exclaim in unison.

Madeline challenges their thinking again. "I wonder if the zero will happen more often? What other amounts might have no pennies?" This idea is difficult. Although several children can see that fourteen is made up of ten and four—or one ten and four extras—and that twenty is made up of two tens, can they extend this idea to other numbers? To really understand place value, a reflective abstraction needs to occur—that is, the pattern they are noticing has to be extended from these specific cases to numbers in general (Piaget 1977).

expand their thinking

Ellie offers another conjecture. "I think maybe thirty. Probably ten, twenty, thirty, forty, fifty, sixty, seventy, eighty, ninety, and a hundred have no pennies."

"So now we can check out Ellie's conjecture. Look what you started, Roland!" Madeline smiles warmly at Ellie and Roland and they beam back.

What Is Revealed

This glimpse into Madeline's classroom reveals a very different approach to mathematics from the one most of us experienced in our past schooling. Traditionally mathematics has been perceived as a ready-made discipline to be handed down by a teacher skilled in the art of transmitting, or explaining, clearly. In the classrooms most of us have attended, teachers stood at the chalkboard and explained place value, many of them using only the symbols and words. Some may have used base-ten blocks or bundled straws to explain how ten objects became one ten; a few may even have introduced games like Chip Trading, hoping that making these transactions would lead

traditional view of Mathematics

X-mania

innovative

• must construct meaning

"mathematizing"

to an understanding of place value. But the premise was always the same. The teacher was the fountain of wisdom who understood that mathematics was a discipline thought to comprise facts, skills, concepts, formulas, and algorithms, and this discipline could be transmitted, explained, practiced, and learned if teachers were well versed in it and learners were diligent. Most students in mathematics classrooms did not see mathematics as creative, but instead as something to be explained by their teacher, then practiced and applied. One might call this traditional view "school mathematics."

Mathematicians, on the other hand, engage in quite a different practice. They make meaning in their world by setting up quantifiable and spatial relationships, by noticing patterns and transformations, by proving them as generalizations, and by searching for elegant solutions. They construct new mathematics to solve real problems or to explain or prove interesting patterns, relationships, or puzzles in mathematics itself. The renowned mathematician David Hilbert once commented that he liked to prove things in at least three or four different ways, because by doing so he better understood the relationships involved. At the heart of mathematics is the process of setting up relationships and trying to prove these relationships, mathematically, in order to communicate them to others. Creativity is at the core of what mathematicians do.

Interestingly, the sculptor Henry Moore described his work in much the same way Hilbert did. He said that before he sculpted, he always drew something several times to learn more about it. In fact, we all find ways to make meaning from our interactions in the world. The process of constructing meaning is the process of learning. We actually create our knowledge; we do not discover it. Writers make meaning when they formulate stories and narratives, when they construct characters and plots, when they play with words and metaphors. Scientists make meaning by wondering about scientific phenomena, by hypothesizing, designing, and performing experiments, and then by proposing explanations to fit their results. Musicians hear cadence, rhythm, harmony, discordance, and melody as they interact in their world; artists see color, form, texture, and line.

In fields other than mathematics, we've understood this constructive nature of learning. We teach students to become good writers by involving them in the process of writing. In science, we engage learners in actively inquiring, in formulating hypotheses, and in designing experiments. We teach art by allowing learners to create it. Have we traditionally been teaching mathematics in our classrooms or only the "history" of mathematics—some past mathematicians' constructions and their applications? Is there any connection at all between "school mathematics" and "real mathematics"?

The vignette from Madeline's classroom is evidence of a different view of mathematics—one more closely akin to the process of constructing meaning—that might be better termed "mathematizing." Children are organizing information into charts and tables, noticing and exploring patterns, putting forth explanations and conjectures, and trying to convince one another of their thinking—all processes that beg a verb form. This view of mathematics was put forth by the well-known twentieth-century Dutch mathematician Hans Freudenthal (1968) when he argued that mathematics was a human activity—the process of modeling reality with the use of mathematical tools.

To generate such mathematizing, Madeline immerses her students in an investigation grounded in context. As they make "architectural drafts" of the intended jewelry and complete charts to be used when selling the items, they notice numerical patterns in their data. They explore these patterns and try to figure out why they are happening. Throughout the process, they raise their own mathematical questions and discuss them in the mathematical community of their classroom. But is this only process? What about content? Do all the children construct an understanding of place value? Is place value even the goal that day for all the children?

Back to the Classroom

Let's go back to Madeline's classroom on a day prior to the one on which the children are discussing the pattern Roland notices. On this day, Cathy Fosnot, a Mathematics in the City coteacher, is also in the room. Cathy is sitting with Tara and Sarah, who are making a drawing of a red-and-green necklace that will have twenty-two beads.

Sarah is carefully counting each bead on her drawing. So far, she has drawn three groups of five—five red, five green, then five red. She counts by ones, tagging each bead with her finger, and saying one number for each bead, in synchrony with her touch. When she gets to fifteen, she draws four new green beads one at a time on the same side of the necklace saying, "Sixteen, seventeen, eighteen, nineteen."

Tara interrupts her. "You need more than that, and you need five of each color."

Sarah adds another green bead and then, rather than saying, "Twenty," counts all the beads from one again until she reaches twenty. Then she draws two more green beads on the other side and says, "Twenty-one, twenty-two. There. We're done."

Sarah's counting strategy of returning to one, rather than counting on from nineteen, is typical of many young children. To understand that nineteen is inside of twenty, that numbers are nested inside of each other (like Russian nesting dolls), and that the difference grows by one each time is another big idea for children (Kamii 1985). They must construct, first, the idea that *twenty* means twenty things. They see adults in their environment count to see "how many." And although children can copy these actions and learn the singsong of counting, they do not necessarily understand that the result of the counting represents an amount. Even when this idea is constructed, it is still a big leap for them to infer that $20 = 19 + 1$.

Tara has constructed these ideas. She explains to Sarah that nineteen beads are not enough—she knows that nineteen is inside of twenty-two. Sarah, on the other hand, is in the midst of constructing these ideas. She counts by ones as she works, and when interrupted by Tara, she cannot retain the nineteen and count on. Nor does she look at the beads and count by fives to recapture the amount. She must start over again, from one.

Cathy wants these girls, particularly Sarah, to think about the amounts. One way to do this is to have them consider the relation between the number of pennies and the number of beads. Another is to have them consider the groups of fives nested within the twenty-two beads. Skip counting by fives would be more efficient than recounting from one. To that end, Cathy hands the girls an ink pad and coin stamps (penny, nickel, and dime) and asks them to figure out how much they should charge for the necklace. What should the customers pay? Then she moves to another section of the room, where Madeline is working with Graham and Ellie.

Graham and Ellie are drafting their necklaces with Unifix cubes and laying them out in a line. They are working next to a hundreds chart. Ellie exclaims, "Hey, Graham, I found another one . . . 16! See?" She lays out a train of Unifix cubes: five brown, five yellow, five brown, one yellow.

"Yeah, that's another one that fits your rule," Graham acknowledges. "My rule's the opposite," he explains to Madeline.

"What do you mean by the opposite?" Madeline inquires.

"Well, because I didn't have trouble with twenty," Ellie interjects.

"And I did have trouble with twelve," Graham finishes. "See? When you attach the twelve together into a necklace [*he takes a Unifix train of five yellow, five brown, and two yellow and lays it in front of Madeline*] you get seven yellow in a row. Trouble!"

Graham and Ellie have become intrigued with the idea that some amounts, when made into a necklace, will not follow the pattern of groups of five. For example, twelve beads, when turned into a circular necklace, will not work. The five yellow on one side and the two yellow on the other will become seven yellow in a row when a circle is made. The pattern of fives will be lost (see Figure 1.1a). A necklace of twenty, however, forms a per-

FIGURE 1.1a
*Graham's Idea: Necklaces
that will be "trouble"*

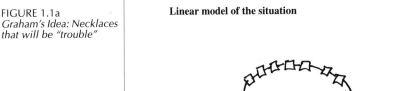

Linear model of the situation

becomes seven yellow

Circular model of the situation

fectly alternating "groups of five" necklace. Ellie is interested in the amounts that will keep the pattern of fives intact, with at least one bead of a different color breaking up the groups (see Figure 1.1b).

Madeline begins to understand. "Oh, you mean when you tie the real necklace together, the yellow will look like seven instead of five and two?"

"Yeah." Graham raises his hands, palms turned out, and shakes his head in an exasperated fashion, obviously intrigued by the dilemma.

"Then how is your rule the opposite, Ellie?" Madeline asks.

Ellie points to the hundreds chart, "Ten, twenty, thirty, forty, fifty, sixty, seventy, eighty, ninety, one hundred. All these numbers won't be trouble."

"Why won't they be trouble?"

"Maybe because they're all even numbers," Ellie ponders. "I think here [*she points to 21, 31, 41, 51, 61, 71, 81, 91*] . . . these are all odd. I bet we'll have trouble."

Ellie notices an odd/even relation and offers it as a possible explanation of why some numbers might work. Although it is of course true that all the perfect necklaces are made up of even numbers (10, 20, 30, etc.), the reverse is not true: all even numbers do not make perfect necklaces, nor do they even make necklaces that fit Ellie's rule. Yet as is often the case, even a wrong idea can provide a powerful mathematical insight. Thus, talking about ideas—the social community of mathematicians—can be instrumental in fostering the development of knowledge. Such is the case here. As Ellie puts forth her insight, Graham picks up on it; they scaffold their ideas, each upon the other's.

"Yeah!" Graham exclaims. "The odd fives when you put them together won't look good, because you get another number. But the even ones, when you put them together . . . you won't get into trouble!"

Note the language Graham uses: "odd fives." Ellie had mentioned odd numbers, not odd fives. His insight into this problem is amazing. He is not only able to consider the fives as groups of five, he is able to consider the *number of groups* as even or odd! For a five-year-old, this is brilliant mathematics—a beautiful, elegant creation.

And now Ellie picks up on this idea and creates an even more encompassing solution. "Hey, I just figured something else out! With numbers

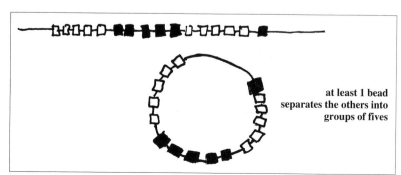

**at least 1 bead
separates the others into
groups of fives**

FIGURE 1.1b
*Ellie's Idea: Necklaces
that won't be "trouble"*

ending in five, four, three, two, or one, you'll always have trouble, but with six, seven, eight, nine, and ten, you'll never have trouble!"

"Wow, that's an interesting conjecture, Ellie! Check it out and keep me posted. I'll be back." Madeline is exuberant over the mathematics these two children are doing, but she knows they need time to explore further. If she acknowledges their solution now as correct, they will accept her word for it and stop thinking. To really understand, learners must work out their ideas thoroughly. They must be able to prove relationships to themselves and to their peers. And, as Hilbert said, it's even more powerful to prove it several ways!

Madeline also admittedly wants time to explore for herself the mathematics involved in Ellie's and Graham's conjectures. Children's inquiries often take them on a journey the teacher has not yet explored! This is often the case with mathematicians, too: one's questions spur another to investigate. Rather than feeling anxious over the new mathematics that arises, we can enjoy the investigation as well. We should view our role not as the provider of answers, but as the facilitator in learning. We can plan, but also partake in, the journey of constructing ways to mathematize our world. Madeline makes a note to herself to work on this conjecture of Ellie's and Graham's that night, then her eyes roam across the room to ensure that all twenty-seven students are involved in their work. Since everyone seems to be, she sits down to listen in on the conversation of three other children.

Cathy returns to Sarah and Tara. They have stamped four nickels and two pennies on their drawing of the necklace with twenty-two beads. Responding to a question from Cathy, Tara demonstrates with her fingers the groups of five, saying, "One five, a second five, a third five, a fourth five. So customers have to give us four nickels and two pennies."

"Oh, I see. That makes sense." Cathy acknowledges her agreement with the girls' thinking, noticing with interest that Tara is counting by fives and then counting the groups. But what about Sarah? She seems to agree with Tara, since she is nodding, but it is often difficult for a teacher to know whether *each* child really understands. To give Sarah more time to grapple with Tara's ideas, Cathy suggests they figure out what customers would pay if they used dimes. She leaves the girls to work on that question, then she visits Raul and Pete. They have drawn a necklace of fifteen beads. Cathy asks them how they know it is fifteen.

Pete explains, skip counting by fives: "Five, ten, fifteen."

However, Cathy sees that although the boys have stamped three nickels on their drawing, they have also stamped ten pennies alongside the nickels, for a total of thirteen coins. She asks them how much money that is, commenting that it looks like an expensive necklace for only fifteen beads.

Raul counts the coins by ones, "One, two, three, four, five, six, seven, eight, nine, ten, eleven—"

Cathy stops him at eleven, pointing to the nickel. "How many beads is the nickel for?" she asks. "The nickel is worth five cents, isn't it?"

Pete and Raul seem unperturbed by Cathy's question, acknowledging the nickel is worth five cents but still counting eleven, twelve, thirteen. Cathy tries several other questions to bring out the unitizing, but she is unsuccessful and the boys begin to lose interest.

TEACHING AND LEARNING AS DEVELOPMENT

As Madeline and Cathy wander from group to group, their questioning changes in relation to what the children are investigating and in relation to the ideas each child is in the midst of constructing. Although place value is the overall "horizon"—a general goal purposely embedded in the context by Madeline—each child is at a different place developmentally, and therefore the context is also open enough to allow for individual exploration and divergence. Asking Tara and Sarah to figure out the cost gives them the opportunity to revisit the quantity of twenty-two. Sarah has originally counted by ones, even starting over when she goes from the nineteenth to the twentieth bead. The coins can become a "constraint" to counting by ones and therefore may facilitate the development of counting on, skip counting, or unitizing (i.e., five cents is also one group of five).

Since Ellie and Graham are already able to unitize, Madeline's questions center on the patterns they have noticed in relation to odd and even groups of five and leftovers. As they continue their explanations, they are actually dividing various amounts into fives, and Madeline hopes they may be able to construct the relationship between even groups of five and groups of ten.

In both these instances, the learning seems smooth. The children's inquiries bring wonderful mathematical opportunities to the fore, and the teachers' questions seem to be helpful. Learning—real learning—is not always so smooth, however, as the dialogue with Pete and Raul demonstrates. Although Cathy tries to provoke disequilibrium in relation to their scheme of counting the nickels as ones, she is unsuccessful. The boys are not yet capable of making the connection between one nickel and five beads. Or perhaps they can (they do represent the three groups of five with three nickels), but their understanding falls apart when they try to consider the whole of fifteen. It is also possible they understand unitizing but are simply counting coins. Often the best questions are those that simply illuminate the learner's thinking, but in the middle of teaching this is hard to remember. Teachers tend to focus, lead, or ask questions in relation to their own (the teacher's) agenda—and Cathy falls prey to that tendency here.

Even so, all the children are immersed in an investigation that involves mathematizing. And more than process is happening. Children are exploring ideas such as quantity, unitizing, and division, in relation to their own level of mathematical development. And mathematizing should not be dismissed as simply process. Mathematizing *is* content. As children learn to recognize, be intrigued by, and explore patterns, as they begin to overlay and interpret experiences, contexts, and phenomena with mathematical questions, tools (tables and charts), and models (the linear Unifix train vs. the

[margin annotations:]
children are at different paces / leads to individual exploration

★ *important!*

} becoming mathematicians

circular necklace), they are constructing an understanding of what it really means to be a mathematician—to organize and interpret their world through a mathematical lens. This is the essence of mathematics.

Madeline supports her students by posing questions and offering rich contexts for mathematizing. This approach enables children to take the next step in the learning process. The development of the children seems to guide Madeline's teaching. But development can be nothing more than a catchword. No one would disagree that development is important. Educators have talked about developmentally appropriate practice for years. But what does development *in relation to mathematics learning and teaching* mean?

Madeline's teaching reflects her appropriate understanding of development. But she does more—she employs a different framework. Her teaching is grounded in the development of *mathematical ideas*—in her knowledge of the structure of mathematics. But still there is more. She understands the paths and the horizons of the landscape of this learning; she knows how children *come to understand* different mathematical ideas. She thinks about how to employ *mathematical contexts* as a didactic—how to use them to facilitate mathematical learning. She knows and recognizes important landmarks along the way—strategies, big ideas, and mathematical models—and she designs her contexts with these landmarks in mind. Different contexts have the potential to generate different models, strategies, and big ideas.

Madeline journeys with her students. In her framework, learning and teaching are connected. She works on the edge between the structure of mathematics and the development of the children; the value she gives each differs with what happens in her classroom.

STRATEGIES, BIG IDEAS, AND MODELS IN A TEACHING/LEARNING FRAMEWORK

Strategies as Schemes

The mind is never a blank slate. Even at birth, infants have organized patterns of behavior—or schemes (Piaget 1977)—for learning and understanding the world. Beginning as reflexes (grasping and orienting, for example), these initial schemes soon become differentiated and coordinated. Children learn to crawl and then walk to objects to be grasped, felt, sucked, and explored visually. Grasping is refined to include pushing, pulling, hitting, and other forms of exploring with the fingers. Sucking is differentiated into chewing, biting, and licking. New strategies for exploration are constructed.

Children attempting to understand "how many"—how many plums there are in the grocer's box, how many stairs they have climbed, how many fish there are in the fish tank—use various assimilatory schemes. They hold up three fingers to show perceptual correspondence; they line up objects one to one; they count (often double-tagging some objects). Sometimes they count the same objects over and over again (when counting fish in the fish tank, for example)! Eventually they learn to tag and count each object once and only once, and they learn to count on. These strategies in turn evolve into strategies for addition and subtraction, counting backward, skip counting, and taking leaps of ten.

Developing all these strategies is no mean feat! The progression of strategies, or "progressive schematization," as we like to call it (Treffers 1987), is an important inherent characteristic of learning.

Big Ideas as Structures

Underlying this developmental progression of strategies is the construction of some essential big ideas. What is a "big idea" and how is it different from a strategy? Big ideas are "the central, organizing ideas of mathematics—principles that define mathematical order" (Schifter and Fosnot 1993, 35). As such, they are deeply connected to the structures of mathematics. They are, however, also characteristic of shifts in learners' reasoning—shifts in perspective, in logic, in the mathematical relationships they set up. As such, they are connected to part/whole relationships—to the structure of thought in general (Piaget 1977). In fact, that is *why* they are connected to the structures of mathematics. As mathematical ideas developed through the centuries and across cultures, the advances were often characterized by paradigmatic shifts in reasoning. These ideas are "big" because they are critical to mathematics and because they are big leaps in the development of children's reasoning.

For example, *unitizing* is one big idea we saw children grappling with in Madeline's class. Unitizing underlies the understanding of place value; ten objects become one ten. Unitizing requires that children use number to count not only objects but also groups—and to count them both simultaneously. The whole is thus seen as a group of a number of objects. The parts together become the new whole, and the parts (the objects in the group) and the whole (the group) can be considered simultaneously. If we know the number of beads in a necklace and how many beads are in a group, we can figure out the number of groups, or the number of nickels, dimes, and pennies to charge. For learners, unitizing is a shift in perspective. Children have just learned to count ten objects, one by one. Unitizing these *ten* things as *one* thing—one group—requires almost negating their original idea of number. It is a huge shift in thinking for children, and in fact, was a huge shift in mathematics, taking centuries to develop.

Shift in thinking

Models as Tools for Thought

Language was constructed to signify meaning. When we construct an idea, we want to communicate it: through time and across cultures humans have developed language to do so. Initially, language represents ideas and actions; it is *a representation of thought*. Eventually it serves as *a tool for thought*.

Numerals were developed to signify the meaning of counting. Operational symbols like + and − were constructed to represent the actions of combining and comparing. While these symbols were initially developed to represent mathematical ideas, they become tools, mental images, to think with.

To speak of mathematics as mathematizing demands that we address mathematical models and their development. To mathematize, one sees, organizes, and interprets the world through and with mathematical models. Like language, these models often begin as simply representations of situations, or problems, by learners. For example, learners may initially represent a situation with Unifix cubes or with a drawing, as the children did when they drafted their necklaces. These models of situations eventually become generalized as learners explore connections between and across them. As Graham and Ellie modeled the necklaces linearly and then circularly, they were puzzled because of the "tension" between the models. Then they shifted to a generalized notion of number, employing the numerals on the hundreds chart to continue their inquiry. Using numerals to signify their original models, they further mathematized their understanding of the situation. The hundreds chart became a tool to think with.

Teachers can use models as a didactic to bridge learning from informal solutions specific to a context with more formal, generalizable solutions— to bridge models *of* thinking with models *for* thinking (Beishuizen, Gravemeijer, and van Lieshout 1997; Gravemeijer 1999).

using models

Walking the Edge

Madeline walks the edge between the structure of mathematics and the development of the child by considering the progression of strategies, the big ideas involved, and the emergent models. Ultimately what matters is the mathematical activity of the learner—how the learner mathematizes the situations that Madeline designs. But learning—development—is complex. Strategies, big ideas, and models are all involved—they all need to be developed as they affect one another. They are the steps, the shifts, and the mental maps in the journey. They are the components in a "landscape of learning."

Strategies, big ideas, and models, however, are not static points in a landscape. They are dynamic movements on the part of a learner in a journey of mathematical development. From this perspective they need to be understood as schematizing rather than as strategies, as structuring rather than as big ideas, and as modeling rather than as models (Freudenthal 1991). Teaching needs to facilitate this development. Only then can teaching and learning be seen as interrelated—for the connected teaching/learning framework that it is. This is the framework behind Madeline's decision making.

teaching + learning

SUMMING UP . . .

Look again at the epigraphs to this chapter. "It's the questions that drive mathematics. Solving problems and making up new ones is the essence of mathematical life. If mathematics is conceived apart from mathematical life, of course it seems—dead." When mathematics is understood as mathematizing one's world—interpreting, organizing, inquiring about, and constructing meaning with a mathematical lens, it becomes creative and alive. "The mathematician's patterns, like the painter's or the poet's, must be beautiful. . . . There is no permanent place in the world for ugly mathematics."

Traditionally mathematics has been taught in our schools as if it were a dead language. It was something that past, mostly dead, mathematicians had created—something that needed to be learned, practiced, and applied. When the definition of mathematics shifts toward "the activity of mathematizing one's *lived* world," the constructive nature of the discipline and its connection to problem solving become clear.

Shift in mathematics

When we define mathematics in this way, and teach accordingly, children will rise to the challenge. They will grapple with mathematical ideas; they will develop and refine strategies as they search for elegance; they will create mathematical models as they attempt to understand and represent their world. Because this process of mathematizing is constructive, teachers need to walk the edge between the structure of mathematics and the development of the learner. This edge is a journey across a landscape of learning that comprises strategies, big ideas, and models. From the perspective of mathematics as mathematizing, it is the mathematical activity of the learner that ultimately matters; thus, strategies, big ideas, and models need to be understood as schematizing, structuring, and modeling. Teaching needs to be seen as inherently connected to learning.

Children, in learning to mathematize their world, will come to see mathematics as the living discipline it is, with themselves a part of a creative, constructive mathematical community, hard at work.

2 | THE LANDSCAPE OF LEARNING

*It is not knowledge but the act of learning,
not possession but the act of getting there,
which grants the greatest enjoyment. When
I have clarified and exhausted a subject,
then I turn away from it, in order to go into
darkness again; the never satisfied man is
so strange. . . . If he has completed a structure, then it is not in order to dwell in it
peacefully, but in order to begin another. I
imagine the world conqueror must feel thus,
who, after one kingdom is scarcely con-
quered, stretches out his arms for others.*

—*Karl Freidrich Gauss*, Letter to Bolyai

DESCRIBING THE JOURNEY

Linear Frameworks

Historically, curriculum designers did not use a developmental framework like Madeline's when they designed texts, nor did they see mathematics as mathematizing—as activity. They employed a teaching/learning framework based on the accumulated content of the discipline. They analyzed the structure of mathematics and delineated teaching and learning objectives along a line. Small ideas and skills were assumed to accumulate eventually into concepts (Gagné 1965; Bloom et al. 1971). For example, simplistic notions of fractions were considered developmentally appropriate for early childhood if they were taught as a shaded part of a whole or with pattern blocks. Later, around third grade, the equivalence of fractions was introduced, and still later, in fifth or sixth grade, operations with fractions. Development was considered but only in relation to the content: from simple to complex skills and concepts. *true!*

Focusing only on the structure of mathematics leads to a more traditional way of teaching—one in which the teacher pushes the children toward procedures or mathematical concepts because these are the goals. In a framework like this, learning is understood to move along a line. Each lesson, each day, is geared to a different objective, a different "it." All children are expected to → *traditional math* understand the same "it," in the same way, at the end of the lesson. They are assumed to move along the same path; if there are individual differences it is just that some children move along the path more slowly—hence, some need more time, or remediation. Figure 2.1 depicts such a linear framework.

Learning Trajectories

As the reform mandated by the National Council for Teachers of Mathematics has taken hold, curriculum designers and educators have tried to develop other frameworks. Most of these approaches are based on a better understanding of children's learning and of the development of tasks that will challenge them. One important finding is that children do not all think the same way. These differences in thinking are obvious in the dialogue in Madeline's classroom. Although all the children in the class worked on the "Grandma's necklace" problem, they worked in different ways, exhibited different strategies, and acted in the environment in different mathematical ways.

Marty Simon (1995) describes a learning/teaching framework that he calls a "hypothetical learning trajectory." The learning trajectory is hypothetical because, until students are really working on a problem, we can never be sure what they will do or whether and how they will construct new interpretations, ideas, and strategies. Teachers expect their students to solve a problem in a certain way. Or, even more refined, their expectations are different for different children. Figure 2.2 depicts a hypothetical learning trajectory.

FIGURE 2.1
Linear framework

FIGURE 2.2
Hypothetical learning trajectory

Simon uses the metaphor of a sailing voyage to explain this learning trajectory:

> You may initially plan the whole journey or only part of it. You set out sailing according to your plan. However, you must constantly adjust because of the conditions that you encounter. You continue to acquire knowledge about sailing, about the current conditions, and about the areas that you wish to visit. You change your plans with respect to the order of your destinations. You modify the length and nature of your visits as a result of interactions with people along the way. You add destinations that prior to the trip were unknown to you. The path that you travel is your [actual] trajectory. The path that you anticipate at any point is your "hypothetical trajectory." (136–37)

As this quote makes clear, teaching is a planned activity. Madeline did not walk into her classroom in the morning wondering what to do. She had planned her lesson, and she knew what she expected her students to do. As the children responded, she acknowledged the differences in their thinking and in their strategies, and she adjusted her course accordingly. While she honored divergence, development, and individual differences, she also had identified landmarks along the way that grew out of her knowledge of mathematics and mathematical development. These helped her plan, question, and decide what to do next.

must make adjustments

Over the last five years, the Mathematics in the City staff have been helping teachers like Madeline develop and understand what we originally called "learning lines"—hypothetical trajectories comprising the big ideas, the mathematical models, and the strategies that children construct along the way as they grapple with key mathematical topics (number, place value, addition and subtraction, and so on). In conjunction with these teachers, we analyzed children's work, we looked at videotapes of lessons, and we interviewed children. We discussed the *strategies* (and their progression—the schematizing) that children used as they acted within the environment mathematically. We attempted to specify the important *big ideas* the children grappled with for each topic. And we focused on *mathematical modeling,* whereby students see, organize, and interpret the world mathematically.

Although we still believe that knowledge of models, strategies, and big ideas will enable teachers to develop a "hypothetical learning trajectory," we have stopped calling it a learning line—the term seems too linear. Learning—real learning—is messy (Duckworth 1987). We prefer instead the metaphor of a landscape.

The big ideas, strategies, and models are important landmarks for Madeline as she journeys with her students across the landscape of learning. As she designs contexts for her students to explore, her goal is to enable them to act on, and within, the situations mathematically and to trigger discussions about them. Madeline also has horizons in mind when she plans—horizons like place value or addition and subtraction. As she and the children move closer to a particular horizon, landmarks shift, new ones appear.

The paths to these landmarks and horizons are not necessarily linear. Nor is there only one. As in a real landscape, the paths twist and turn; they cross each other, are often indirect. Children do not construct each of these ideas and strategies in an ordered sequence. They go off in many directions as they explore, struggle to understand, and make sense of their world mathematically. Strategies do not necessarily affect the development of big ideas, or vice versa. Often a big idea, like unitizing, will affect counting strategies; but just as often "trying out" new counting strategies (like skip counting) they have seen others use will help students construct unitizing. Ultimately, what is important is how children function in a mathematical environment (Cobb 1997)—how they mathematize.

It is not up to us, as teachers, to decide which pathways our students will use. Often, to our surprise, children will use a path we have not encountered before. That challenges us to understand the child's thinking. What is important, though, is that we help all our students reach the horizon. When we drive a car down the road, our overall attention is on the horizon. But we also see the white line in the middle of the road and use it to direct the car in the right direction. Once that line is behind us, however, it no longer serves that purpose. It is the same with teaching. When a child is still counting all or recounting from the beginning, the teacher designs activities to develop counting on or skip counting, as Cathy did with Sarah. However, when a child understands skip counting, when it seems that landmark has been passed, the teacher has already shifted the landmarks on the horizon to counting in groups or to unitizing, as Madeline did with Roland.

When we are moving across a landscape toward a horizon, the horizon seems clear. Yet we never actually reach it. New objects—new landmarks—come into view. So, too, with learning. One question seemingly answered raises others. Children seem to resolve one struggle only to grapple with another. It helps to have the horizons in mind when we plan activities, when we interact, question, and facilitate discussions. But horizons are not fixed

horizons are constantly changing

FIGURE 2.3
Landscape of learning

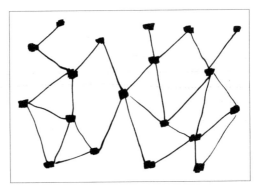

points in the landscape; they are constantly shifting. Figure 2.3 depicts the landscape-of-learning framework.

The learning-and-teaching landscape is a beautiful painting. But is it more metaphoric than real? If learners can take so many paths and the horizons are constantly shifting, how do teachers ever manage? How do we help each child make the journey and still keep in mind the responsibility we have for the class as a whole? The role of context and the development of a classroom community are critical components to consider as we answer these questions.

THE ROLE OF CONTEXT

Word Problems vs. Truly Problematic Situations

One could argue that the use of context in mathematics teaching is not new. Certainly we all have vivid memories of word problems. Usually, however, our teachers assigned them after they had explained operations or formulas, and we were expected to apply these algorithms to the problems. In Madeline's class, context is not being used for *application* at the end of a unit of instruction. It is being used at the start, for *construction*. Nor is the "Grandma's necklace" context a trivial, camouflaged attempt to elicit "school mathematics." It is a rich, truly problematic situation that is real to the students, that allows them to generate and explore mathematical ideas, that can be entered at many levels, and that supports mathematizing.

Much reform is currently underway in schools in accordance with the new National Council for Teachers of Mathematics (NCTM) *Principles and Standards for School Mathematics* (2000), and many teachers, rather than teaching by telling, are attempting to use problems to facilitate construction. But many of the problems teachers introduce are still traditional word problems. Join us in another classroom, and we'll show you what we mean.

Meg, a second-grade teacher, is reading a problem from a sheet to five children grouped around her. "Jane is making bracelets . . ." She turns to the children. "Do you want me to read it, or do you want to?"

Several of the children chorus, "You."

Meg continues. "Jane is making bracelets. She has seventy-nine beautiful glass beads to use. She uses ten beads for each bracelet. How many bracelets can she make?" She pauses, thinks about what she has read, and then although it is not part of the original problem, adds, "And how many beads left?"

Meg begins by involving the children in solving a problem. She is not asking them to apply an algorithm, but instead she asks them to think—to solve the problem in a way that makes sense to them. She is attempting to promote construction, not application. She is clear about the mathematics (place value) she wants the children to explore, and she structures the context to support development, just as Madeline did. But could Meg's context be stronger? Do the children become invested in the problem? Do they mathematize it?

One of the children, Sean, starts to take a handful of base ten materials out of a nearby bin, then puts them back, commenting, "Oh, I don't need these, easy." Other children comment that they are confused. One of these children, Jason, questions, "Ten in every bracelet? What kind of bracelets?"

Meg attempts to clarify the confusion. "Complete bracelets. Look at my question. 'How many bracelets could Jane make?' And complete would mean ten beads. . . ." She pauses, then adds, "And obviously there is one bracelet that isn't complete. I wouldn't ask the question otherwise."

This "bracelet" story is a scenario children can imagine (they have probably strung beads before), and in that sense it is realistic. But it is not likely to promote mathematizing. It is not likely to cause children to interpret their "lived world" on the basis of mathematical models. It is closed, with an expected answer of "seven with nine beads left over"—a camouflaged attempt at eliciting 79/10 = 7 r 9. Why must there be ten beads in a bracelet? Bracelets are usually made by size, not quantity of beads. And even if one accepts that ten and only ten are needed in a bracelet, is the answer seven bracelets, or eight bracelets with one incomplete? No wonder there is initial confusion when Meg reads the problem. In real life, the remainder needs to be considered, and taken care of. Instead, the problem is designed around "school mathematics." Because the children are confused, Meg must clarify. She attempts to steer the children toward the place value pattern that she wants them to notice by adding the question, "How many beads in the bracelet that isn't complete?" Unfortunately, now there is almost nothing left to solve, since the children are told that one bracelet won't be complete. The context becomes irrelevant, and the children will sacrifice their own meaning making to accommodate what Meg wants.

Two children respond, "Oh, that's easy." A third, Julie, remains confused.

Meg repeats the problem. "Think about it. Jane has seventy-nine beads to make some bracelets. She has to put ten beads in each bracelet. How many bracelets can she make?"

Julie quickly says, "Oh, six—no, seven."

At first Meg does not acknowledge the correctness of her answer, responding, "Think about it, because you'll have to tell me how you figured it out, won't you?"

But Julie's confusion is still apparent. "I don't get it."

"Okay." Meg attempts to give Julie more time. "Jason is going on to think of another way to figure it out. Maybe the rest of you would like to find another way, too, while we give Julie more time to think about it."

Julie responds with more conviction, "Seven . . . because ten goes into seventy-nine."

This time Meg acknowledges her thinking. "Okay, that is seven bracelets, so how many in the bracelet that isn't complete?"

Meg is patient as she reminds Julie that she will have to explain her thinking. She does not supply an answer, nor does she acknowledge the correctness of Julie's first solution—that would stop her from thinking. To give Julie the time she needs, Meg encourages the other children to work on

[handwritten margin note: Problem ☹]

[handwritten margin note: giving students time]

encouraging use of other strategies

another strategy. But is the problem rich enough to benefit from exploring alternative strategies? What alternative strategies are there?

Teachers often confuse tools with strategies. Unifix cubes or base ten blocks or paper and pencil are not different strategies. They are different tools. Representing the problem with stacks of Unifix cubes grouped into tens, or with base ten blocks, or by writing "10" seven times are all the same mathematically. No benefit is derived by changing tools unless the new tool helps the child develop a higher level of schematizing (in this case, moves the child from counting by ones to employing repeated addition of tens). Is this context rich enough for that?

teachers often confuse tools w/strategies

Meg turns to all the children and invites them to begin a discussion. "Who would like to explain how they figured it out? And I would like the rest of you to listen, and if you have a question, ask."

Julie offers to begin. "If there are seventy-nine beads, and if you used ten in each bracelet . . . [*she counts base ten rods as she continues*] ten, twenty, thirty, forty, fifty, sixty, seventy, so that would be seven. How many were in the bracelet that isn't finished? Nine. These [*she points to the unit cubes*] are only nine, not ten. And each of these [*she points to the rods*] is a group of ten."

Meg points to the rods and acknowledges Julie's statement. "These are groups of ten." Then she turns to Sean. "Sean, you did it without cubes . . . you started to take them and then put them back. Can you explain what you did?"

"Yeah, you just take the seven from the tens and put it down. The tens are more over here [*he points to the tens column*]. So I just knew seven bracelets. Then you take the nine from the ones. So you take the nine and put it there."

Note the language Sean uses: "take the seven from the tens, take the nine from the ones." He treats the problem totally abstractly. He already knows the mathematics, and the context is irrelevant. The strategies explained thus far are either counting by tens or knowing the mathematics already. Let's look at a few more responses.

"So you just knew that the seven meant seven tens?" Meg rephrases. "Any other different ways? Jason?"

Jason's strategy is similar to Julie's. He also counts by tens. "There were seventy-nine beads and the seventy beads . . . each one of those was a ten [*he uses his fingers to demonstrate*] so . . . ten, twenty, thirty, forty, fifty, sixty, seventy. Each of those was a bracelet [*he holds up seven fingers*]. The nine was left over. I put it there."

Meg asks, "Did you just know that, but use your fingers to prove it?" Jason acknowledges that he just knew. Meg then turns to Nancy, who comments, "I just knew, too." Meg concludes the lesson with, "That's something that is really neat about our number system, remembering that the seven stands for seven tens. It makes it easy to use."

When a context is real and meaningful for children, their conversation relates to the context. They mathematize the situation. They talk about bracelets and beads, necklaces and coins. There are a variety of strategies that children use. Mathematical questions arise.

Context, real + meaningful

good context +

Noticing how children are thinking about a problem, noticing whether they stay grounded in the context, tells the teacher whether the context is a good one or not. When the context is a good one, the children talk about the situation. When it is a camouflaged school-mathematics problem, children talk about number abstractly; they lose sight of the problem as they try to figure out what the teacher wants.

Madeline's context had the potential for genuine mathematizing as children employed linear and circular models for their necklaces and as they generated tables delineating the money customers would pay. Patterns appeared in the data on the table, and these patterns triggered additional explorations. In contrast, the context in traditional word problems quickly becomes unimportant; children say "seven with nine left" or "seven tens" rather than "seven bracelets." And once they have an answer to the "teacher's question," they see ★ no reason to employ alternative strategies or to inquire further.

Finding Situations for Mathematizing

If the goal of mathematics instruction is to enable children to mathematize their reality, then situations with the potential to develop the ability to mathematize need to be carefully designed (or found). To encourage children to become mathematically literate—to see themselves as mathematicians—we need to involve them in making meaning in their world mathematically. Traditionally, we have told young learners that mathematics is all around us— but we have given trivial examples, such as seeing numerals on signs, in telephone numbers, and in addresses or seeing geometric shapes in dishes, cups, boxes, and other objects in our environment.

Situations that are likely to be mathematized by learners have at least three components:

models

1. The potential to model the situation must be built in (Freudenthal 1973). Bus and subway scenarios in which people get on and off can be modeled by adding on and removing—addition and subtraction. Grocery and retail store scenarios, collecting data and finding ways to organize them, taking inventory of materials in the classroom, even board games and card games, all have the potential to develop mathematical modeling.

Realize

2. The situation needs to allow children to *realize what they are doing*. A child drawing a necklace with twenty two beads and determining what coins customers can use to pay for it can picture or imagine the mathematics concretely and can check the reasonableness of answers and actions. The Dutch use the term *zich realiseren*, meaning "to realize in the sense of to picture or imagine something concretely" (van den Heuvel-Panhuizen 1996).

inquiry

3. The situation prompts learners to ask questions, notice patterns, wonder, ask why and what if. Inquiry is at the heart of what it means to mathematize. Questions come from interacting with the world around

us, from setting up relationships, from trying to solve problems. When the problem is "owned," it begins to come alive.

Building in Constraints

Learners' initial informal strategies are not the endpoint of instruction; they are the beginning. As teachers, we must support the development of these initial attempts into more formal and coherent mathematical strategies and models; we must encourage "progressive mathematizing" (Gravemeijer 1999). Although peer discussions and teacher questioning can lead students to restructure their initial ideas, building potentially realized constraints and suggestions into the context is often a more powerful means to that end.

Madeline specified a necklace with five beads of each color and introduced nickels and dimes because five things can often be subitized, or seen as a whole, and because five and ten are important landmark numbers in our number system. She hoped that the grouping of the beads by color would support the development of skip counting, or perhaps counting on from five, rather than counting by ones. Children could count by ones if they needed to, and many did. But the grouping context has the potential to stretch a student's thinking. The coins are an additional potential perturbation. While the beads can still be counted by ones if needed, even though the colors suggest grouping, the coins cannot. The "fiveness" of the nickel is implicit, not explicit. Of course children can still count by ones aloud, or count with their fingers by ones, but the coins, more often than not, introduce "disequilibrium" regarding the strategy of counting by ones. The chart of dimes brought out the place value pattern Roland noticed. Madeline was embedding a didactic into the context, molding it in a sophisticated pedagogical way to encourage children to go beyond their initial strategies.

Open vs. Closed Situations

The Nature of Learning

Real learning is constructive and developmental. As children attempt to make sense of a situation and its context, they interpret, organize, and model it based on the ideas or strategies they have already constructed. They schematize and structure it so that it makes sense. Piaget (1977) called this process *assimilation,* meaning "to make similar." The process of assimilation has often been misunderstood as a *taking in.* Rather, it is an *acting on.* We act on experiences when we attempt to understand them with strategies for interpreting, inferring, and organizing. We build new ideas on old ones, or reformulate old ideas into new ones. This part of learning is *accommodation.*

Learners will assimilate contexts in many ways. In every classroom, developmental differences will affect perceptions and strategies. And any new ideas constructed (as accommodations) will be directly linked in learners' minds to *their* past ideas, because they arise from reorganizing the initial ideas.

In Madeline's class, the students employ any number of ideas, inquiries, and strategies. The goal is not the same for everyone every day, but there is equal opportunity for everyone to learn because the situations and their contexts are so open. The "Grandma's necklace" activity offers many entry points for children, from counting the beads one by one, to exploring odd and even groups of five, to grappling with place value patterns. Cathy and Madeline vary their questions to stretch and support individual children's learning.

Closed situations have only one possible strategy. Everyone is supposed to solve the problem in the same way, and learners are either successful or unsuccessful—they either get it or they don't. Open situations, crafted sophisticatedly with a didactical use of context, allow for and support developmental differences, and thus can facilitate mathematical development for everyone.

Closed v. open [handwritten annotation]

Word Problems and Context Problems

Word problems on the surface appear to be open because it seems that there are many possible strategies to arrive at a solution. But, because they are often designed with little context and with trivialized, "school mathematics" in mind, they are usually closed. They are often nothing more than superficial, camouflaged attempts to get children to do the procedures teachers want them to do—procedures that have little to do with genuine mathematizing. Context problems, on the other hand, are connected as closely as possible to children's lives, rather than to "school mathematics." They are designed to anticipate and to develop children's mathematical modeling of the real world. Thus, they are open, with genuine diverse solutions invented by learners as a result. Further, context problems have a didactic embedded in them: they have potentially realized constraints and suggestions built in, in an attempt to support and stretch initial mathematizing. In this sense, their purpose is to promote the *development* of mathematizing. But is this even enough?

Context-Based Investigations and Inquiries

If genuine mathematizing involves setting up relationships, searching for patterns, constructing models, and proposing conjectures and proving them, then context must be used in a way that simultaneously involves children in problem solving *and* problem posing. Madeline could simply have asked her students to figure out how many beads her grandmother would have left over if she bought a package of thirty-seven blue beads and a package of forty-two yellow beads and made a single necklace in alternating groups of five beads of each color. This is a real situation. Colored glass beads are sold in small packages, and the quantities in the packages are often not the same. Children could mathematize this situation in many ways. They could count; they could make groups of five and skip count, or count the groups; they could combine two groups of five into ten; and so on. A didactic use of context is employed that supports mathematizing because of the pattern of fives. But would children have noticed the place value pattern that Roland noticed? Would Ellie and Graham have noticed the patterns in the odd and even groups of fives?

To allow the students to notice patterns, the situation and its context had to be open enough that patterns in data would appear. Piaget (1977) argued that the setting up of correspondences by learners was the beginning of the development of an understanding of relationships. Constructing a connection, a pattern, or a correspondence between objects fosters reflection. Learners begin to wonder why; they want to explain and understand the connections they notice. By asking the children to make a money chart for selling the necklaces, and by having children draft and explore necklaces of many sizes, Madeline opens the situation to allow genuine investigating. Now it has become an investigation rather than a problem, and the children can begin to construct relationships from the patterns they notice. But still this is not enough.

Madeline must also facilitate the students' questions. As they raise inquiries, Madeline gets excited with them and deliberately gets them to discuss their ideas. She supports their inquiries by giving them time and materials to pursue them. If she had not facilitated this aspect of mathematizing —the problem posing—but instead had relied on a structured series of context problems to be solved (even when carefully scaffolded day by day), she would not have developed in the children the ability to mathematize *their* "lived world." Some children would have been lost along the way as the class as a whole moved from activity to activity, and other children would not have been challenged. Instead, by using context-based *investigations* and by facilitating *inquiry* in relation to them, Madeline involves her children in genuine mathematizing, in being young mathematicians at work.

TURNING CLASSROOMS INTO MATHEMATICAL COMMUNITIES

Knowing the difference between word problems, context problems, investigations, and inquiries, and knowing how to keep them open, helps Madeline support each child. Understanding how to mold contexts is an important didactical tool to stretch children. But understanding the role of context is not enough. Madeline also makes her classroom a community in which her students can investigate and share with one another. Developing a community that supports risk taking and mathematical discussions is another critical pedagogical component for fostering real investigations and inquiries, real mathematizing.

The Edge Between the Individual and the Community

Teaching has two important and very different phases. At home, at night, we prepare for the next day. We replay the day just past, remembering the successes, evaluating the inquiries, celebrating the insights some of the children had, recalling the stumbling blocks and the struggles—all from the perspective of mathematical development, with a sense of the landscape of learning. Although our reflections begin with individual children, as we plan we shift our attention to the community—the whole class. Our intent is to keep everyone in the community moving—to move the community as a whole across the landscape toward the horizon. No matter what path a child is on, no matter where on that path the child is, we want to move that child closer to the horizon. Fortunately, we do not need to plan separate lessons for each child—nor could we. Instead we can focus on the community, thinking of contexts and situations that will be likely to move the community as a whole closer to the horizon. These must be open and rich enough that each community member can enter them and be challenged.

The next day, in class, our role changes dramatically. We become a member of the community. We listen to and interact with the children. We try to understand what each child is thinking. We decide whether to ask for clarification. We pose questions that will cause children to think. We are intrigued with individual inquiries and solutions. We think about how members of the community can help one another, how they can scaffold their ideas upon others' ideas. The night before, we were curriculum designers—designing the environment for the community. In class, we are researchers and guides. We journey with the children.

Therein lies our duality: we are community members, yet we plan for the community. We facilitate conversation around mathematical ideas and strategies for the community to consider. But, as a member of the community, we help develop the norms of what it means to prove something, of what counts as a solution, or a conjecture. We walk the line between the community and the individual.

Facilitating Dialogue

Turning a classroom of some twenty-five individuals into a community is not easy: it's a structure very different from the classrooms most of us attended. Traditionally, dialogue in a classroom bounced from teacher to student, back to the teacher, then to another student. The teacher was there to question and give feedback. She stood at the front of the classroom; the learners sat facing her.

In a "community of discourse" (Fosnot 1989), participants speak to one another. They ask questions of one another and comment on one another's ideas. They defend their ideas to the community, not just to the teacher. Ideas are accepted in the community insofar as they are agreed upon and not disproved. The community develops its own norms for what it means to prove one's argument, for what stands as a mathematical problem, for how data get collected, represented, and shared. As a member of the community (but walking the edge), the teacher facilitates, monitors, and at times provides counterexamples and/or highlights connections to ensure that this dialogue supports genuine mathematical learning.

Dialogue between students can be fostered by ensuring that students are encouraged to speak about each other's ideas. After a student shares an idea, we can ask, "How many of you understand the point Jane made and can rephrase it in your own words?" The students' responses tell us not only how many of them appear to understand but also *how* they understand, how they are schematizing, structuring, and modeling. Discussion cannot happen if the community is not considering the presenter's thinking. Because construction, not transmission, lies at the heart of learning, everyone is responsible for thinking about and commenting on one another's ideas. After several children have paraphrased an idea and we are confident that most students are participating, we can ask follow-up questions like, "Does anyone have a question? Who agrees? Who disagrees? Does anyone have a different idea or a different way of thinking about it?" Questions like these keep the dialogue bouncing from student to student, from community member to community member.

Structuring Math Workshop

Investigations and Inquiries

When classrooms are workshops—when learners are inquiring, investigating, and constructing—there is already a feeling of community. In workshops learners talk to one another, ask one another questions, collaborate, prove, and communicate their thinking to one another. The heart of math workshop is this: investigations and inquiries are ongoing, and teachers try to find situations and structure contexts that will enable children to mathematize their lives—that will move the community toward the horizon. Children have the opportunity to explore, to pursue inquiries, and to model and solve problems in their own creative ways. Searching for patterns, raising questions, and constructing one's own models, ideas, and strategies are the primary activities of math workshop. The classroom becomes a community of learners engaged in activity, discourse, and reflection.

Math Congress

After investigating and writing up solutions and conjectures, the community convenes for a "math congress." This is more than just a whole-group share. The congress continues the work of helping children become mathematicians in a mathematics community. Mathematicians communicate their ideas, solutions, problems, proofs, and conjectures with one another. In fact, mathematical ideas are held as "truth" only insofar as the mathematical community accepts them as true.

In a math congress, young learners—young mathematicians at work—defend their thinking. Out of the congress come ideas and strategies that form the emerging discipline of mathematics in the classroom. The sociocultural aspects of this emerging discipline are directly connected to the community. What holds up as a proof, as a convincing argument? What counts as a beautiful idea or an efficient strategy? How will ideas be symbolized? What is mathematical language? What does it mean to talk about mathematics? What tools count as mathematical tools? What makes a good mathematical question? What serves as a conjecture? All of these questions get answered in the interactions of the community. The answers arise from the sociocultural norms and mores that develop.

Once again we as teachers are on the edge. We must walk the line between the structure and the development of mathematics, and between the individual and the community. As we facilitate discussions, as we decide which ideas to focus on, we develop the community's norms and mores with regard to mathematics, and we stretch and support individual learners. We move the community toward the horizon, *and* we enable individuals to travel their own path.

We can structure math congresses in many ways. If we want to focus on a big idea, we can look for them in children's work and facilitate discussion around them. If we want to illuminate mathematical modeling, we focus discussion on the connections between different solutions and strategies. If we want to help refine strategies, we can scaffold the discussion from less efficient to more efficient solutions. Our goal is always to develop mathematizing—to promote steps and shifts in thinking, to help learners develop mental maps. We focus on the community's journey, yet we work toward each student's construction of meaning.

Minilessons

A description of math workshop would not be complete without a few words about minilessons. Several minilessons are described in this book, particularly in Chapter 8. Often we may want to highlight a certain computational strategy, to share certain problem-solving heuristics, or to discuss what makes a valid proof. A ten-minute minilesson at the start of math workshop is a great way to do so. In a minilesson, we as teachers take a more explicit role in bringing ideas and strategies to the surface. But once again we walk the edge. We put forth ideas for the community to consider, but we must allow individuals to construct their own meaning.

SUMMING UP . . .

Learning and teaching are interrelated; one does not occur without the other. Genuine learning is not linear. It is a messy journey, characterized by many paths and different-sized steps and shifts. Genuine teaching guides learners on this journey, and is directed toward landmarks and horizons. In the epigraph to this chapter we quote the great mathematician Gauss writing to Bolyai, "It is not knowledge but the act of learning, not possession but the act of getting there, which grants the greatest enjoyment." As we learn, we construct. We near the horizon only to have new landmarks appear. Because learning is not linear, teaching cannot be either. If we as teachers have a deep knowledge of the landscape of learning—the big ideas, the strategies, and the models that characterize the journey—we can build contexts that develop children's ability to mathematize. By opening up situations into investigations and facilitating inquiry, we can support children's journeys along many paths.

But we need to walk the line between supporting individuals and planning for the community. Development of the class as a community is critical. In a community, trust and respect are shared by everyone. Traditionally, respect was reserved for the teacher: the teacher spoke, learners listened, and the teacher always had the last word. For a community to function well, all members must respect one another. Everyone's ideas deserve attention, and each person must be trusted to be responsible for the task at hand. Everyone must be trusted to be able to learn. In the beginning of the year, we need to work hard on establishing routines and structures for math workshop. The learners in our classroom must be led to trust that their ideas count, that their peers and the teacher really care about their thinking, that they will be given the time to explore different strategies and pursue their inquiries, that their mathematical insights matter.

But community cannot be divorced from content. Mathematicians talk about mathematical ideas, not feelings or rules of behavior. They respect one another for the mathematical ideas they bring to the discussion. Learners, no matter how young, know the difference between really being listened to and superficial attempts. They know when they are learning and when they are not. They know when what they are doing is interesting, when it matters, and when it is simply about pleasing the teacher. When intriguing contexts are being explored and mathematical "big ideas" are being grappled with, engagement is high. Children can be mathematicians when we give them a chance to mathematize *their* reality and trust that they can.

3 | NUMBER SENSE ON THE HORIZON

Neither in the subjective nor in the objective world can we find a criterion for the reality of the number concept, because the first contains no such concept, and the second contains nothing that is free from the concept. How then can we arrive at a criterion? Not by evidence, for the dice of evidence are loaded. Not by logic, for logic has no existence independent of mathematics: it is only one phase of this multiplied necessity that we call mathematics. How then shall mathematical concepts be judged? They shall not be judged. Mathematics is the supreme arbiter. From its decisions there is no appeal. We cannot change the rules of the game, we cannot ascertain whether the game is fair. We can only study the player at his game; not, however, with the detached attitude of a bystander, for we are watching our own minds at play.

—*Tobias Dantzig,* Number: The Language of Science

The concept of number is the obvious distinction between the beast and man. Thanks to number, the cry becomes a song, noise acquires rhythm, the spring is transformed into a dance, force becomes dynamic, and outlines figures.

—*Joseph Marie de Maistre,* Mathematics Quotation Server

EMERGING STRATEGIES AND BIG IDEAS

Karen During, a preschool teacher in New York City, sits with three four-year-olds playing a board game in which small, multicolored plastic bears are placed on a track, one bear for each square. The board has two tracks so that two children can play. However, the game is played cooperatively, rather than competitively, the goal being to fill both tracks with bears. A large foam die, with faces numbered 1 to 6, is used to determine how many bears to place on a track at a time.

"Inez, you roll the die first. And remember we read the top of the die to tell us how many bears to put on the track."

Inez nods, and rolls a six. Carefully, touching each dot on the upturned face of the die, she counts, "One, two, three, four, five, six."

Acknowledging Inez's counting, Karen says, "Six. So can you count six bears?"

Inez places one bear on each dot, without counting them. Karen calls attention to her strategy. "Look at how Inez is counting the bears. She is putting one on each dot. And now you can put them on the track." Inez places one bear on each square. "So how many bears did you put on the board?" Karen asks, almost as an afterthought.

Surprisingly, Inez does not respond with six. Instead she holds up her hand to show five fingers and then proceeds to count the bears saying, "One, two, three, four, five." Although there are six bears, and she touches each one while she counts, her voice is not in synchrony with her tagging of the bears and she only says five words: one, two, three, four, five. One almost wonders if, because she has said five, she wants to prove it.

not in synchrony

"Five?" Karen queries. She attempts to bring the other two children into the conversation. "Did she put five bears down, Shareema?"

"No, three!" Shareema says.

Inez counts again, this time slowly and purposefully saying one word for each bear that she tags: "One, two, three, four, five, six."

"Six bears!" Karen turns to Shareema. "Is it six, Shareema? Why don't you count them."

Shareema counts, "One, two, three, seven, eight, nine, ten." Although she tags each bear only once as she counts, she says too many words and skips to seven after three.

"My goodness," Karen exclaims. "Did you put ten bears there, Inez?"

Inez shakes her head no, and Shareema counts again, this time slowly and carefully, with one word for each bear: "One, two, three, four, five, six."

Karen asks the third child, Mia, to count. Mia counts each bear only once, and with perfect synchrony says a word each time she tags a bear: "One, two, three, four, five, six."

"So how many are there, Mia?" Karen asks.

Mia leans over and whispers in Karen's ear, "One."

"One?" Karen is incredulous. "How many? Is there only one bear there?"

"No," says Shareema. "There's a lot!"

Struggling with Counting

Preschool teachers or parents of young children are probably smiling with recognition. We are so sure that because children can recite numbers, they understand number. Yet we are proved wrong again and again. What can we tell about children's understanding of number from this vignette, and what is it that makes number so difficult for young children to understand?

Inez lays one bear on each dot on the face of the die as a way to ensure that she has the same amount of bears as dots. While she seems to understand the one-to-one correspondence in her action, and in fact comes up with this strategy as a way to determine the quantity of bears she needs, her action does not transfer immediately to an understanding that the numbers must be the same. In her mind, although the bears match the dots, one for one, it is very possible that the dots can number six while the bears number five. In his long-term study of children's conception of number, Piaget (1965) describes children with similar beliefs. His researchers dealt chips one at a time into two different-shaped beakers, and most young children believed (even though they had watched the chips being dispensed) that the taller, thinner one contained more! The action of dealing one chip at a time or of placing one bear on each dot appears to be little more than a matching activity, with quantity not conserved.

Struggling to Understand "How Many?"

Witnessing the counting struggles of Shareema and Inez, we see how difficult it is for the girls to coordinate their fingers and voices. Although both girls tag each bear once and only once, they do not say the words that correspond to each tagging action. Equally often, children say the correct words when they tag but skip or double-tag pieces. Difficulty with motor coordination may be partly to blame, but the primary reason is that a big mathematical idea is involved here that they have not yet constructed. ★

To know that the number you say tells the quantity you have and that the number you end on when counting represents the entire amount involves *cardinality*—the idea that number means "amount." That "amount" is the same no matter how you arrange it. If you have six dots and match a bear to each, then you necessarily have six bears. Without this understanding, counting is little more than a singsong activity to young children, a rote action they perform when adults ask them to see how many of something there are. They count because they have seen adults do so in this situation, but they don't understand why—it's as if they have learned a script and are acting it out. Shareema counts and gets ten, then counts and gets six. Both are plausible to her. In fact, when Mia says, "One," Shareema does not say, "No, six"; she says, "No, a lot!" The action of her counting to six has little connection to the question of how many.

All children struggle to understand cardinality as they come to see the world through a mathematical lens. No matter what country, what language, this is one of the first big ideas in a young child's mathematical development. Take the following dialogue between Taoufik, a Dutch boy age four, and his teacher.

Teacher: [*Handing Taoufik a box containing seven licorice candies*] How many candies are in the box?

Taoufik: Three.

Teacher: Count them for me.

Taoufik: [*Double-tagging some candies and skipping others*] One, two, three, four, five, seven, eight.

Teacher: [*Smiling*] Yes?

Taoufik: [*Counting again*] One, two, three, four, five, six, nine.

Teacher: Nine?

Taoufik: To nine?

"To nine?" is an interesting response. It's as if Taoufik is trying to understand why the researcher would say nine. He has yet to construct the understanding that the number he ends on, when counting, tells how many there are. He has yet to construct cardinality.

We see this same lack of understanding of cardinality and one-to-one correspondence in the following vignette from Diane Jackson's class of four-year-olds (Cameron and Jackson 1998). Diane has just asked how many containers of milk she needs for the fourteen children present in class that day. The children are well aware that each child gets one carton of milk at snack time. Yet look at their responses.

"So how many milks should I get for fourteen children? Tanaya?"

"Five."

"Tanaya says we need five milks for fourteen children." Diane repeats Tanaya's response and juxtaposes it with the number of children as she paraphrases, hoping some children might notice the numbers. "Tarik, what do you think?"

Tarik too is undeterred by the mention of fourteen. "Six," he says.

"Leroy, how many milks do you think we need for fourteen children?"

Leroy doesn't respond with equivalence either, although he errs on the side of more rather than less. "Seventeen."

"Tyrone, how many milks do you think we need for fourteen children?"

"All of them."

Diane is surprised by this response. "What?"

"All of it," he explains.

"What do you mean, Tyrone?" Diane probes.

"All the milks."

There are no milk cartons in the room, so Tyrone is not referring here to an amount. Apparently, he wants to be sure that everyone gets one. In the past when "all the milks" have been passed out, everyone got one. He does not know how many this amount is, however, and he makes no correspondence to the number of children. None of the children questioned see a relationship between the number of milks and the number of children.

On the other hand, small amounts, such as two, three, or four, can often be seen as a whole (subitized). Young children can perceive the amount without needing to count. Babies at six months will become habituated to a display of three objects and treat a new display of four as novel; they will also be surprised if one object is added to two and three does not result (Wynn 1998). Many birds can also tell the difference between two, three, and four. If a nest contains four eggs, one can be taken safely, but when two are removed the bird generally deserts (Dantzig 1930; Guedj 1996).

Does this mean babies and birds do understand cardinality, at least with small amounts? Let's visit Karen's classroom again. She is playing the same game, but this time with Mia and a new partner, Andrea, also age four.

Andrea rolls a four and places two green bears and two yellow bears on the board, carefully counting and pointing to each. "I have one, and I have two, and I have three, and I have four," she sings happily as she places the bears on the track.

[handwritten margin note: Tyrone is making NO correspondence]

Mia rolls a three and puts three green bears down.

Karen asks, "Who has more?"

"I do, I do, I do!" Andrea exclaims without counting.

"Who has more green bears?" Karen asks.

"I do!" Mia tosses her hair and grins at Andrea.

Andrea takes away her two yellow bears and replaces them with two green bears. "Now I do," she retorts proudly.

What is notable here is that Andrea and Mia can compare two, three, and four bears without counting and understand the *magnitude* of each group. They know which group has more even without counting. They seem in this case to be perceiving the whole, rather than determining or inferring quantity. Recall Mia in the earlier (by ten minutes) episode, in which she counted to six and said she had one bear! It appears that subitizing is more perceptual than mathematical, and that the idea of magnitude is much easier for children to construct than cardinality.

But if one knows that a group of three is more than a group of two, doesn't one understand number? And even if a child understands that the number she ends on when counting represents the total amount, is that sufficient evidence to say she understands number? Let's look at another interview, this time with Stephano, also age four. The interviewer is Willem Uittenbogaard, a researcher at the Freudenthal Institute in the Netherlands and a faculty member of Mathematics in the City.

Willem gives Stephano a box containing seven licorice candies and asks, "How many do you see?"

Stephano organizes them in the box and counts, tagging each one and synchronously saying, "One, two, three, four, five, six, seven."

Willem asks, "Seven candies?" Stephano nods and Willem continues, "So now I'll take one out." He places it on the table and puts the cover back on the box. "How many are in the box now?"

Stephano looks puzzled. He closes his eyes and tries to conjure up a mental image of the inside of the box and counts softly, "One, two, three . . . three!"

"Three?" Willem asks. "Let's look."

Stephano looks into the box Willem has reopened and counts again, "One, two, three, four, five, six . . . six candies!" he exclaims.

Willem checks for cardinality, "So how many are in here now?"

Stephano replies confidently and with an understanding of cardinality, "Six!"

"So now I will take another one out." Willem places the second candy on the table and covers the box again. "How many in here now?"

Once again Stephano attempts to count a mental image. He whispers, "Four, five, six . . . ," then out loud exclaims, "four!"

"This is difficult, isn't it?" Willem acknowledges Stephano's struggle. "So now I'll put them all back." He takes the two candies from the table and places them in the box. "How many are in here now?"

"Five!" Stephano guesses.

Stephano understands that the result of his counting will tell how many

[handwritten margin note: magnitude easier to understand than cardinality]

hierarchical inclusion (handwritten margin note)

candies there are. He understands that seven means seven things, an amount—cardinality. Yet he is unable to infer that if one candy is removed from this group of seven, six remain; that when one more is removed from six, five remain; and that when the two taken out are replaced, the original total of seven results. He has yet to construct *hierarchical inclusion* (Kamii 1985; Piaget 1965)—the idea that numbers build by exactly one each time and that they nest within each other by this amount. This mathematical big idea requires a logical inference, an operation on the whole. If one more is added to five to get to six, then necessarily when one is removed from six, five remain. The ability to maintain the whole amount (six) and to understand how the parts, in this case five and one, are related to the whole requires an operation. Children (and birds, for that matter) can perceive two or three as a whole (subitize) without doing any mathematical thinking. We can perceive three objects as a group of three and know it is more than two because it looks like more, without performing a mathematical operation on it. But to understand that when we count to nine (e.g., an amount too large to subitize) the result is nine objects, and that if one is removed there are eight objects left because eight and one more make nine, requires logical, mathematical thinking.

harder when it requires mathematical thinking (handwritten margin note)

It is this big idea of hierarchical inclusion that gets extended by children into a more complete understanding of number and the construction of two more big ideas, *compensation* and *part/whole relationships*. Once children construct an understanding of hierarchical inclusion, they can begin to consider how if 6 + 1 = 7, then necessarily 5 + 2 = 7 as well, because while one more has been removed from the six it has been added to the one—compensation. Or to put it in context, if the total thrown by two dice is seven, what are all the possibilities that could exist on each die? As this idea of compensation is extended to generate other ways to make seven, a deeper understanding of parts to the whole is constructed. Here the logic is that if 5 + 2 = 7, then necessarily 7 − 2 = 5. If two is on one die and the total is seven, then the number on other die must be five.

IDENTIFYING LANDMARKS

Strategies, like synchronic counting/tagging and counting on, and big ideas, like one-to-one correspondence, cardinality, hierarchical inclusion, compensation, and part/whole relationships, are important landmarks in the landscape of learning for early number development. Without understanding these landmarks, children asked to figure out how many cookies there will be all together if one child brings in eight and another brings in two will count three times. First they will use their fingers or cubes to count out eight; then they will count out two; and finally they will put the two amounts together and recount it all again from one! Counting on is a very difficult strategy for children to construct, because they almost have to negate their earlier strategy of counting from the beginning. And understanding *why* the strategy works depends on developing a sense of cardinality and hierarchical inclusion. Further, without understanding part/whole relationships and compensation, children asked how many seven cookies and three more cookies are (or if there are ten cookies and we eat two, how many are left) make no connection between this subsequent problem and the initial problem of 8 + 2. Instead, they solve it once again by counting three times.

These landmarks in the mathematical environment epitomize children's struggles in their journey toward the horizon of number sense. These landmarks should inform our decision making as teachers because they characterize the shifts and steps in early mathematical development. Some of these landmarks may even become "horizons" in the journey toward numeracy. But it is important that they do not become goals devoid of context. They are not a series of flags or signposts to be reached and checked off, like a list of objectives. Instead, when we plan, we should try to design environments that are likely to enable children to mathematize in ways characteristic of the landmarks. The focus should be on articulating "the nature of the mathematical environment in which we hope students will eventually come to act" (Cobb 1997).

The relationship between the landmarks—between big ideas and strategies—is reciprocal. Sometimes the construction of a big idea like hierarchical inclusion will change a child's counting-from-one strategy to counting on. At other times, the construction of a strategy like counting on may bring about an understanding of part/whole relationships. Number sense is the horizon, but the closer we get to it, the more it begins to change. New landmarks appear.

DESIGNING CONTEXTS

Knowing the landscape enables us to design activities and contexts to foster real learning. But how are we to proceed? Just as children learn to crawl, walk, and talk at different ages, so too does their mathematical development proceed differently. An early childhood class will include students who have not yet constructed cardinality, those who count with double-tagging, and those who are beginning to construct the concepts of hierarchical inclusion, compensation, part/whole relationships, and counting on. When one recognizes this developmental nature of learning, one sees the fallacy in the belief that one activity or series of activities can bring all children to the same point at the same time. Contexts must be chosen and/or designed that allow for these individual differences. Games, routines, and planned investigations can all be used in the early childhood classroom.

Using Games

Children of all ages, across all cultures, love to play games. Board games, card games, and dice games provide rich contexts for mathematical learning. The one caution here is to downplay competition as much as possible. Young children have a difficult time understanding the role of probability, chance, and luck in relation to games and thus take losing personally. With slight *goal — collaboration not competition*

modifications, most games can easily be turned into collaborative activities. For example, the "bear tracks" game that Karen During was playing with Shareema, Inez, Mia, and Andrea is most often played competitively—the goal is to see who can finish a track first. With a slight twist in directions—the goal is to fill all the tracks—the game can become collaborative. The goal of many card games is usually to be the first player to run out of cards; this can be altered to continue play until everyone is out of cards, with children allowed to help one another. Board games with only one series of squares to move along can also be continued until all players finish.

Board Games

good point

Almost any board game in which players move along a series of squares, whether commercial (Candyland, Chutes and Ladders, etc.) or homemade (e.g., Bear Tracks), has the potential to bring up rich mathematical moments for young children. If we are aware of the strategies and big ideas inherent to the development of an understanding of number and have identified where each child is on his or her path toward these horizons, we can orient our use of games accordingly, varying our questions to provoke mathematical thinking in relation to each child's development.

Revisiting the dialogue that occurs as Karen plays Bear Tracks with her students, we see this is what Karen does. When Inez says she has placed five bears down on the track after matching six bears to six dots, Karen asks Shareema and Mia what they think. She attempts to provoke disequilibrium by getting all three girls to consider whether there are six, five, ten, or three bears (or even only one bear) on the track. Shareema and Inez do correct their counting during this discussion. However, this one episode does not develop cardinality, nor is that the goal for each child.

When a child is learning to walk, a few steps may be taken on one day and a few falls the next. Yet the caregiver keeps presenting opportunities for the child to try. Learning is a messy business; constructing understanding is hard work. These young children are trying to figure out what number is all about. Karen appreciates that struggle and simply tries to bring up opportunities for them to consider cardinality. Working with a child who has constructed an understanding of cardinality but not of hierarchical inclusion or part/whole relationships, Karen might, after the second roll, ask the child how many bears there are all together or ask how many more bears are on one track than on the other.

Card Games

Card games can also be used as contexts to promote mathematizing. Kamii (1985) describes how the simple game of War can be turned into a mathematically rich experience. She renames the game More. Let's listen in as Cathy Fosnot changes the rules slightly and teaches the game to Julia and Susie (both age five).

Cathy deals out one card to each girl in turn from a regular deck of cards (minus the face cards). Aces remain and count as ones. (Cathy has opaqued the extra suit symbols near the numerals so that the number of clubs, hearts, spades, or diamonds on each actually matches the numeral.) She says while dealing, "One for Julia, one for Susie, one for Julia, one for Susie," until all forty cards are dealt. When she finishes, she ponders, "Hmm, do you think it's fair? Do you each have the same number of cards?" Julia begins to count hers.

Cathy asks her to wait: "Before you count, what do you think?"

"I think yes," Susie posits. "Because you gave one to Julia, and one to me, one to Julia . . . like that. Unless you made a mistake."

"What do you think, Julia, about what Susie said?" Cathy asks, attempting to get Julia to consider one-to-one correspondence in relation to the resulting amounts, but Julia just shrugs. "Do you want to check?" Both girls check by counting. Julia struggles after fourteen, and Susie helps her. They report that they each have twenty.

"See," Susie says with a toss of her head, "I was right. And you didn't make a mistake!" She smiles at Cathy.

"Okay, so let's play." Cathy begins to explain the game. "Here's how you play. Julia, you turn over a card, and then, Susie, you do too. And we see which is more." Julia turns over a six of clubs, Susie, a five of hearts. "Which is more?" Cathy inquires.

Both girls respond in chorus, "Six." (Even children who cannot read the numerals can play this game. They can count the objects on the cards and compare them. Even if they double-tag or are not counting synchronously, they can match one for one. Also, they often correct each other.)

"How do you know that six is more than five?" Cathy probes.

Susie shows with her finger how there is one heart for every club but that there is one extra club. Julia agrees and explains, "When you count you go past five to get to six. One, two, three, four, five, six. So six is more."

Cathy continues to explain the game. "So six beats five, and we'll put both cards in the six bag." Cathy has provided ten small paper bags, labeled with the numerals from one through ten. Using the bags lessens the sense of competition, but it also brings out the idea of hierarchical inclusion: each bag will capture only numbers contained within the amount specified by the numeral on the bag.

Play continues. Julia turns over a ten of diamonds. "Wait." Cathy stops Susie from turning over her next card. "Before you go, do you think you can beat that?" Cathy wants to encourage the children to think about hierarchical inclusion, not just to count.

Both girls think. Julia slowly begins to smile, "No, because ten is the biggest in here!" Susie agrees and turns over a six of diamonds. Both cards are placed in the bag labeled *10*.

Play continues until all the cards are played. Then the bags are examined to see what numbers were beaten by the numeral labeled on the bag.

"Hey, the one bag has no cards!" Julia exclaims.

"Because one is the littlest. It can't beat anybody," Susie explains.

Julia continues exploring the bags. "Four doesn't have any cards either."

"Could it?" Cathy asks.

"It could have beaten three," Julia responds.

Susie completes the inclusion sequence. "And two and one! How come it didn't?" She opens other bags. "Oh look, here's some fours. There's one in the five bag, two in the eight bag, and one in the ten bag."

 Questions asked while these games are being played can facilitate the development of particular ideas and strategies: in the vignette above, Cathy focuses hers on hierarchical inclusion. But the games themselves can also be varied. The More game can be turned into Double More: instead of turning over one card each, each player turns over two cards and the sum determines the winner. Questions asked while playing this version might stretch children to count on or to construct the idea of compensation. For example, if one child turns over a seven and a two, and the other child's first card is a six, before the fourth card is played we might ask, "What do you need to get to beat nine? How do you know?"

Dice Games

There are many dice games on the market that will prompt children to grapple with mathematical ideas. Once again, familiarity with the landscape of learning enables powerful questioning. Games can also be made that will bring certain mathematical ideas to the surface for exploration. Cathy developed one called Part/whole Bingo for a kindergarten class in New Paltz, New York. Each player has a game card with tracks of various lengths drawn on it (see Figure 3.1). Two regular game dice are rolled and the total is called

FIGURE 3.1
*Part/whole bingo game
boards with Unifix cubes*

out. Players must use that number of Unifix cubes either to cover a single track that matches the total or to cover two or more smaller tracks that add up to the total. Tracks must be covered completely in a single turn. For example if 6 and 4 are rolled, totaling 10, ten cubes must be used. One player might choose to cover the 10 track with them; another might choose instead to cover 2 and 8; or a third, 2, 2, 3, and 3. The objective is to cover the whole board, as in bingo. Although young children often begin by counting out the cubes and covering up only the track matching the total, they quickly begin to see that if they break up the whole into other parts, they will be able to cover more tracks. Part/whole relationships begin to surface. Even children who struggle to count can play, because after they count the Unifix cubes they must lay them on the corresponding track(s), and children help and correct each other. To avoid competition, play continues until all the game cards are filled.

[margin note: part/whole relations]

Even a simple made-up game like Cover-up can present wonderful mathematical dilemmas for young children. Tom O'Brien played this game with Jared, age five. Tom placed five chips in front of Jared. After Jared determined that there were indeed five chips, Tom asked Jared to close his eyes. While Jared's eyes were closed, Tom placed his hand over two chips. When Jared opened his eyes and saw the three remaining chips, Tom asked him to think about how many chips were under his hand. Jared guessed four. Tom showed him the two under his hand and they tried a few more rounds, but Jared's answers seemed to be only guesses with no strategy in place for figuring out the covered quantities. Tom then suggested they switch roles, with Jared covering some when Tom had his eyes closed. To Jared's amazement, Tom's answers were always correct. "Wow, you must have X-ray vision!" he exclaimed, unable to imagine any other way to explain Tom's answers.

Cover-up is a wonderful game to play with a group of children. If a few of the children have constructed hierarchical inclusion and counting on, they can figure out how many are covered. The other children will be both puzzled and amazed by how their friends know and will struggle to figure out their strategy. Such puzzlement and intrigue engenders learning.

Using Routines

Common routines such as taking attendance or lunch count, setting up for snack, passing out materials, and the like are potentially wonderful situations for fostering an understanding of number. By themselves, however, these routines do not automatically produce learning. Talking about how many days of school have occurred and writing the numerals (for example, 23 because 22 was written yesterday) or taking attendance as a group by counting—both common practices in many early childhood classrooms—may produce little or no learning. Children who do not understand cardinality are merely being led to count to the teacher's answer, and children who have constructed the concepts of cardinality and hierarchical inclusion probably don't need the activities. In the words of Eleanor Duckworth (1987), "Either they know it already and I'm too late, or I'm too early and they can't learn it anyway."

Instead, teachers need to turn these situations into real, open dilemmas that beg to be mathematized while still allowing for individual developmental differences. We need to think deeply about the role of context. Ginger Hanlon, a participant in the Mathematics in the City program, received a fellowship to teach in a preschool program in London for a year. During that time she kept a detailed journal. The following annotated excerpts (Hanlon 1996) show how teachers can turn everyday routines into rich problematic situations that use context didactically. In Hanlon's class, three "class helpers" determined whether there was enough snack for everyone before it was passed out.

> Each morning I gave the helpers a sheet containing facsimiles of the snack item that I had on hand or that had been brought in that day, in the quantity available. I asked them to help me determine whether or not there were enough snacks to serve one to each classmate present that day. Supplies at the table where we worked included paper, pencils, and Unifix cubes.

Ginger purposely does not place the real snacks on the table. If she did, the helpers would most likely just pass them out. There would be no need to model the problem mathematically; the action would be sufficient. Instead, she develops a context with a constraint—representations of the snack items. The children have to think about how to model the problem mathematically, with cubes or in a drawing.

> On this particular day, Dean (age five), Yasia (age five), and Robert (age four) were seated at the table with me, each with a photocopied sheet that contained pictures of 22 biscuits. The biscuits were arranged in 5 rows—4, 5, 5, 4, and 4, respectively, from top to bottom.

Ginger arranged the biscuits in rows to see whether any of the children would subitize the amounts and count on, rather than counting by ones. She also wanted to see how the children would organize their counting. Would they start on the top of the page and work to the bottom so as to be sure that they didn't count any twice? Or would they just randomly count and become confused about where they had started?

> Dean immediately began to count the biscuits to himself. He started at the top left of his page and counted from left to right, top to bottom (double-tagging once) and announced that there were 23 biscuits. Yasia said, "I'll check," and began to count her sheet, left to right, top to bottom, systematically. Robert counted his sheet, more randomly but along with her. Yasia reached 22, and Robert stopped counting when she did and agreed with her. Dean then said, "We have too many biscuits. We've got at least twenty of them because

they got twenty-two and I got twenty-three . . . so we must have too many." Dean knew that there were never more than 19 children in our class and so he concluded, because he has constructed hierarchical inclusion, that 22 or 23, whichever is correct, was sufficient. Dean then recounted his sheet and agreed as well that there were 22 biscuits.

Once children have constructed the concept of cardinality, they naturally double-check themselves and recount more carefully when they get different answers. This brings tagging and counting in synchrony to the surface. Here, although Dean has originally double-tagged, he corrects himself, aware that both answers cannot be correct.

I asked, "Are you sure we have enough?" Dean confidently said yes, but Yasia and Robert were not sure. Yasia said, "Yes, no, yes, oh I don't know." Robert sat and shrugged his shoulders. When I asked how we could make sure, Yasia suggested using the cubes. "What will you do with the cubes?" I asked. Yasia, using red cubes, and Dean, using brown, began to put cubes on each of the biscuits on their sheets. Robert decided to give a cube to each child in the classroom, and began to search for orange cubes to hand out.
Dean finished placing his cubes on his biscuits and then began to count them, moving each cube off the biscuit as it was counted. Yasia left the cubes on the biscuits and counted again to 22. She said, "Maybe we'll have three extra." She then noticed that Robert had not finished handing out his cubes. She asked if he had given them to individual children, naming them, and then helped him check that he hadn't forgotten anyone. "Did you give them to the kids in the block area?" she asked. Once satisfied that he had handed out all the cubes, Robert sat down at the table again. Yasia prompted him to go and collect the cubes and count them. Robert did, placing his cubes in a train on the table. He counted them and announced, "Fifteen."

The children mathematize the situation by modeling it with cubes. Although Dean appears to understand hierarchical inclusion from the start (he comments that whether it is 22 or 23, there are at least 20, and that is enough), Yasia and Robert are not so sure. As they work out the problem, they find their own ways to set up a one-to-one correspondence. In the next part of the transcript they lay their trains next to each other, in a sense modeling, and making use of, two number lines.

I asked, "Well, now what do we do? Do we have enough biscuits?" Again, Dean immediately said, "Yes, we do. Twenty-two is more than fifteen." Robert looked confused, and I asked him if he knew what Dean meant. He shook his head, and I asked if he knew how he could use the cubes he'd collected and Dean's cubes to figure it out. Again he shook his head, and Yasia, before I could say anything, said, "Robert, you've got the kids and I've got the biscuits. If my train is longer than yours, then we have enough." She took her red cubes off the sheet and put them into a long train." It's awful long, isn't it?" she commented. Once she had compared the two trains [see Figure 3.2], she announced that her train of biscuits was longer than Robert's train of kids and so we had enough. I asked if we had enough left over for the adults. Yasia counted the cubes through the fifteenth one and then, holding the train at that point (but covering some of the cubes as she did so), announced that we had four extra. Dean disagreed, and I asked if there was a way to find out for sure how many extra we had. Yasia immediately began to break up her chain of red cubes (biscuits) and tried to place them on top of each cube in Robert's train of orange cubes (children). I said, "What are you doing, Yasia?"

"I'm putting the biscuits on the children to see if we have any left over." Experiencing difficulty getting them to stay on, she enlisted Robert's help in holding them and said to Dean, "Here, Dean, you have a go." She let him place some of the cubes on top of the train. They kept falling off. Yasia then decided to put her red cubes underneath the train. Again she got Robert to hold one end of the "children" train as she placed the individual cubes underneath it. I suggested she put the two trains side by side, reminding her how she had recorded her solution once before by drawing children each with a cube in hand to represent the biscuit they would get.

Although Yasia and Robert model the problem first with two trains of cubes, which allows them to compare the lengths, Yasia's hand obscures some of the leftovers. They solve this dilemma by pairing orange and red cubes (see Figure 3.3). Robert, left to his own devices, might have given up. But Yasia, in her collaboration with him, supports his growth by labeling the cubes *biscuits* and *kids*. He is then able to understand the one-to-one pairing and to see that the seven cubes left are leftover "biscuits."

"What if you put the red cube for the biscuit on top of the orange cube, as if you were holding it?" I said, demonstrating. Yasia immediately began to break up Robert's train of cubes and fit them to the red cubes, again enlisting Robert's aid. In the meantime, I asked

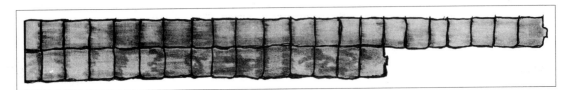

FIGURE 3.2 *Making trains to compare 22 biscuits to 15 children*

Dean, who was quite sure we had enough biscuits and told me sotto voce that we had enough for the adults as well, to find a way to record what Yasia and Robert were doing. Yasia announced, as she placed the cubes, a red atop an orange, in a line, "This is going to be a pattern, isn't it, Ginger?"

It's important to note how real this problem is to the children. They are talking about biscuits and children, not just numbers. They are finding ways to model the problem that allow them to solve it and to conclude that there are seven leftover biscuits, enough for the adults, too!

Many routine situations can give rise to mathematizing. Diane Jackson and Toni Cameron, from New York City, studied the daily routines in Diane's pre-K class as part of their research for the Mathematics in the City program, looking at ways to structure these routines and pose questions in connection with them in a way that would heighten learning (Cameron and Jackson 1998). For example, each day they investigated whether the students in class that day would be able to go in pairs, hand-in-hand, to lunch; thus, the children investigated odd and even numbers every day. Each day they also figured out how many cartons of milk would be needed for snack and took a survey having to do with what children were wearing (e.g., how many children have on red today? is that more than yesterday or less?).

Let's reenter Diane Jackson's pre-K class later in the year as they once again discuss how many cartons of milk are needed for snack, in order to compare the children's current understanding with their earlier responses. This time after they suggest how many cartons of milk are needed, Diane has them pass out cardboard replicas of that number of cartons to see whether they have enough.

"So you wanted sixteen, Leroy? Okay, here are sixteen milks." Diane gives Leroy sixteen cardboard replicas. "I wonder, do you think he will have enough for everyone today?"

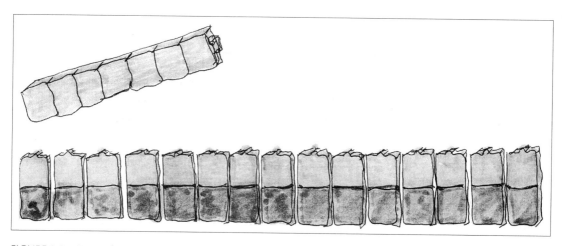

FIGURE 3.3 *Putting biscuits on the children*

Murmured yeses and nos are heard. Leroy places a milk replica in each pocket in the attendance chart that contains a paper doll (which indicates that child is in attendance). Seventeen pockets contain dolls, and the number 17 has been written next to the chart to indicate the day's attendance.

"One," pipes up Jordan.

"What did you say, Jordan?" Diane asks.

"One didn't get one," he explains.

"Yes, one person didn't get a milk." Diane acknowledges Jordan's thinking. "So is sixteen enough for everybody?"

Leroy responds, "No, I need to give Amari a milk."

Diane doesn't give him another replica immediately. Instead she asks, "Well, how many more do you need?" Then she directs her question to all the children, "How many more milks does he need?"

They all agree that one more is needed, so Diane gives it to Leroy. He places it in Amari's pocket. "So you had sixteen, and that wasn't enough for everyone. We had to use one more. How many milks did we need, then?" Diane asks them to calculate the total so that they can record the needed number of milks under the attendance record.

Denzel responds, "Enough!"

Diane smiles. "It was enough. How many do you think is enough? We used sixteen, then we had to get one more. How many do you think that is?"

Tarik chimes in, "Seventeen!"

"You think seventeen, Tarik. Well, let's see." Diane lets Denzel check. He counts out seventeen and agrees with Tarik.

"How did you know it was seventeen, Tarik?" Diane probes.

"Cause seventeen is up there." He points to the attendance chart.

"So if we see seventeen here, we know it's seventeen milks? I wonder why? Why do you think that is?" Diane probes further, trying to engage other children as well.

"'Cause it's seventeen children . . . "

"Tarik says there are seventeen children. So if there are seventeen children, then we need. . . ?"

"Seventeen milks!" Tarik explains, confidently.

Tarik's understanding of cardinality and one-to-one correspondence is distinctly different from the understanding he demonstrated in the earlier episode in which he thought six milks might be enough for fourteen children. By having the children calculate attendance and record it just before they discuss the number of milks they need, Diane has turned a routine situation into one in which the relationship of milk cartons to children is likely to be noticed and pondered. She also prompts the students to check out their conjectures, thereby facilitating disequilibrium.

Designing and Using Investigations

Situations in children's real lives can be wonderful contexts for investigations likely to elicit mathematizing. It is important, though, to think about how to structure the context of these "found" situations in order to facilitate development, to guide children toward new landmarks. For example, a grocery store is rich with mathematizing possibilities: how many apples in the bin? how many peaches? more peaches or apples? how many more? But look at how the context of this situation can be developed:

> When I was walking to school this morning, I stopped at the grocer on the corner to buy some apples. There were so many kinds, green Granny Smith, red Macintosh, yellow Delicious. They were each packaged ten to a pack, with cellophane over them. I wanted a selection of green Granny Smiths and red Macintoshes, but I didn't want to buy two whole packs. That would be twenty apples! I wasn't that hungry!
>
> I asked the grocer why he didn't make a pack of ten with some red and some green. He said there would be so many ways to make them, like one green and nine reds, or five reds and five greens, and so on, that he got confused trying to think of all the ways and had just made all the packs the same! I started wondering, too. How many ways? I told him that I taught a K–1 class in the school down the road and that we would be happy to investigate all the ways and draw some plans up for him. He was so grateful that he gave me a sample box. See, it has two rows. Five apples fit in the top row, and five fit in the bottom row.

Developing a story about two kinds of apples in a box of ten and using a box that has two rows of five builds a structure into the context that has the potential to bring up part/whole relationships and compensation. As children set out to make plans for the grocer, and as they investigate all the combinations, they often begin to construct the idea that as one Granny Smith apple is gained, one Macintosh is lost. Subsequently, you can structure a math congress around this important landmark by asking, "Did anybody find a way to make a box with only one Granny Smith?" On large graph paper, one green square and nine reds can be colored to match the response. The recording process continues with the next question, "Did anyone find a way with two Granny Smiths?" As the recording on the graph paper grows, a staircase evolves (see Figure 3.4) that usually triggers surprise. Students can then explore why the staircase is happening and if it will happen with boxes of other sizes.

A similar activity suggested in many early childhood math books entails rolling ten lima beans from a can onto a sheet of paper and recording how many land on the paper and how many land off. In another version, one side of each lima bean is painted red and children record how many beans land on the red side and how many land on the white side. Although the mathematics is meant to be the same (combinations that add to ten), little more than counting happens in these two versions. Children just count and record. The part/whole relationships and compensation get lost. But even more important, no modeling of the problem, and therefore no mathematizing,

[handwritten margin note: ways to get to 10]

occurs. Investigations need to cause children to raise mathematical questions, to wonder, "Have I found all the ways? How can I be sure?" They need to trigger mathematical modeling.

Investigations can have structures or constraints built into them that will potentially bring some big ideas to the surface, but they also need to have multiple entry points so that they can be challenging no matter where children are in their mathematical development. Just making the box and ensuring that there are ten apples in it stretches young children who are still struggling to count ten objects; others grapple with the part/whole relationships; still others develop a system of exchange to ensure that they have found all the combinations. And as we work with small groups of children, we can vary our questions to stretch each child in a different, developmentally appropriate way.

One final example: Susan Soler, a K–1 teacher for many years, was using TERC's *Investigations in Space, Number, and Data* (1997, 1998). One investigation required that the teacher discuss with the children how many noses there were in the class. The guide suggested that Unifix cubes be passed out, one to each child, and that a tower of cubes be built to demonstrate how many noses there were. After this activity, each child was supposed to draw his or her eyes on an index card, all the cards were to be affixed to a chart, and the class was then to discuss how many eyes there were in the classroom. Susan, having taught for many years and knowing her students quite well, intuitively felt the activity was too closed and would not be challenging. Sure enough, one child even said before any eyes were drawn, "There must be forty-eight, because if there are twenty-five children when everyone is here, that would be fifty eyes, because two quarters are fifty cents. So because Sophia is absent today, there must be forty-eight eyes!" The few children who had not constructed the one-to-one correspondence that would enable them to see that if there were twenty-four children in class there would be twenty-four noses were not challenged by the activity either. If

FIGURE 3.4
The evolving staircase

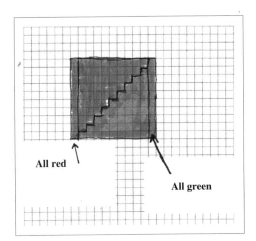

they could not infer *if twenty-four kids, then twenty-four noses,* they could certainly not infer *if twenty-four cubes, then twenty-four noses!* Further, no mathematizing resulted, because the children did not have to conceive of a way to model the problem. The teacher modeled it for them.

When Susan planned the next day's math workshop, she made use of her insights into where the children were mathematically. She opened up the investigation by asking the children to figure out *for themselves, and in their own ways,* how many mouths, how many legs, how many hands, how many fingers and toes. They worked with partners and found their own ways to model and solve the problems, and during their math congress they shared what they had come up with. Susan focused conversation on the connections across solutions. The investigation was now open to multiple strategies, multiple entry points, and various ways to model and mathematize.

SUMMING UP . . .

This chapter has sketched some of the many paths to and landmarks associated with early number sense. This "landscape of learning" comprises the critical big ideas and strategies that children develop—the landmarks they pass—as they construct an understanding of number: strategies like double-tagging and skipping vs. tagging and synchrony when counting, and counting three times vs. counting on when adding. Big ideas such as one-to-one correspondence, cardinality, hierarchical inclusion, compensation, and part/whole relationships must be constructed for children really to comprehend quantity.

If we as teachers become more aware of this "landscape," it becomes easier to find contexts in the lives of students—to open up activities into real investigations involving children in modeling their world mathematically. Games, classroom routines, and real-life situations begin to be seen as potential learning environments, particularly when they are structured in relation to the landscape. As children grapple with mathematical modeling of their world, and as they become puzzled and intrigued by mathematical questions, they begin the real journey of doing and constructing mathematics.

Number sense is a difficult horizon for children. Just as they initially struggle to walk, they struggle to understand this seemingly illusory notion —quantity. There are steps and shifts in thinking along the way. Even when the horizon seems reached, it becomes fuzzy as new landmarks appear. Questions answered only produce new questions *to* answer. But in the words of Joseph Marie de Maistre, in one of the epigraphs to this chapter, "The concept of number is the obvious distinction between the beast and man. Thanks to number, the cry becomes a song, noise acquires rhythm, the spring is transformed into a dance, force becomes dynamic, and outlines figures." As young children construct an understanding of number they take a giant step in learning to mathematize their lived world.

4 | PLACE VALUE ON THE HORIZON

One is hard-pressed to think of universal customs that man has successfully established on earth. There is one, however, of which he can boast—the universal adoption of the Hindu-Arabic numerals to record numbers. In this we perhaps have man's unique worldwide victory of an idea.

—*Howard W. Eves,* Mathematical Circles Squared

Numbers have neither substance, nor meaning, nor qualities. They are nothing but marks, and all that is in them we have put into them by the simple rule of straight succession.

—*Hermann Weyl, quoted in* Armchair Science Reader

ADDITIVE NUMERATION SYSTEMS

How do we comprehend and communicate "how many?"? Although the eye can often perceive five or fewer objects as a whole (see Chapter 3), amounts larger than this need to be counted, or the larger amount needs to be decomposed into smaller amounts that can be subitized and then added. Because we cannot "see" quantities larger than four or five as a whole but instead must operate on them to determine how many, humans across cultures and over time constructed ways to represent amounts symbolically. We invented numerals and operations.

Sticks, Stones, and Bones

The first numerical marks that we are aware of in history come from the Paleolithic era. These marks were slashes, or tallies, carved onto cave walls or into bone, wood, or stone. One slash meant one object; thus ten reindeer were denoted with ten tallies. The marks had a one-to-one correspondence with the objects being counted. Bones bearing such numerical slashes have been found that are nearly 30,000 years old (Guedj 1996).

Because a "one thing, one notch" system was too cumbersome to represent large amounts, over time humans refined this system. One refinement was the use of knots arranged along cords, in Persia, in the fifth century B.C.

(Guedj 1996). By the thirteenth century the Incas had refined this system, developing a *quipu*—a cord held horizontally from which knotted strings hung. The type of knots used, the length of the cord, and the color and position of the strings all communicated levels of quantities: single units, tens, and hundreds. Some cultures used different-shaped stones to represent different amounts, while others made objects out of clay. Sumerian clay stones known as *calculi* (*calculus* is Latin for stone) have been found that date to the fourth millennium B.C. A small clay cone was used to represent a value of one; a ball, ten; and a large cone, sixty. When a contract specifying a particular amount was agreed upon, the calculi representing the sum of that number were placed inside a hollow ball. Notches representing the calculi inside were made on the surface of the seal (Guedj 1996).

Almost all these early number systems used ones, fives, tens, and twenties, but when one realizes that early counting was usually done with fingers and toes, this isn't so surprising.

The Invention of Numerals

The first written mathematical symbols of which we are aware appeared in early Babylonian times (around 3300 B.C.). A nail shape represented units, a chevron shape represented tens. Nine nails and one chevron thus represented nine and ten, the quantity 19. Over time and across cultures, similar written systems were developed. Although new symbols were invented to show quantity groupings, rather than single units, the number of shapes drawn was still in a one-to-one correspondence, either to units or number of groups. And different symbols were used for different-sized groups. For example, the Mayans used a bar to equal five and a dot to represent units. They wrote 19 with three bars and four dots. Ancient Egyptians used lines to represent ones, a basket handle to represent tens, a coiled rope to represent hundreds, and a lotus flower blooming on its stalk to represent thousands. They wrote 19 with one basket handle and nine lines. All of these systems are examples of additive numeration. The operation of addition is employed; the value of the number is equal to the sum of the values of the symbols. Each symbol is repeated the number of times it must be added (Guedj 1996).

Roman numerals are also considered an additive numeration system, in that the symbols represent the worth of the group of objects and the total amount is the sum of the symbols. C represents one hundred; L, fifty; X, ten; V, five; and I, one, and these symbols are repeated the number of times they must be added. One advance exists in this system, though: placing smaller-quantity symbols *before* larger-quantity ones denotes subtraction. That is, XI denotes addition ($10 + 1 = 11$), but IX denotes subtraction ($10 - 1 = 9$). This saved a little of the tedium and cumbersome writing when many symbols were needed to represent large amounts. Nevertheless, even with these advances in the writing of numbers (which took thousands of years), the simplest calculation remained arduous.

The Invention of Place Value

In early numeration systems, the value of the digit had little or no relation to the position in which it was placed. Even in the roman numeral system, although placement could denote subtraction, I still meant one, whether it was placed before or after the X. C always equaled one hundred no matter where it was placed: MCI meant one thousand one hundred and one; MCCCI meant one thousand three hundred and one. The amounts designated by the symbols were simply combined.

The positional notation that characterizes our number system today was a big idea in the evolution of number systems. The idea employs the operation of multiplication. For example, the digit 2 in the second column to the left stands for two tens, but when placed in the third column to the left, it stands for two hundreds. No separate symbols are needed to represent tens or hundreds.

The numerals 1 through 9 appeared in India in inscriptions from the third century B.C., but the symbol for none, and the idea of zero, had yet to be invented. The combination of positional notation and the idea of zero in India in the fifth century A.D., which passed via the Arabs to Europe, produced a powerful new system of notation, one that led to advances in calculating and to the development of modern mathematics. In the ninth century the Arab mathematician Muhammad ibn Musa al-Khwarismi wrote a book, *The Book of Addition and Subtraction by Indian Methods*, presenting these new ideas. The book became extremely famous in Europe and was eventually translated into Latin in the twelfth century, thus establishing column arithmetic, using borrowing and carrying, as the method of calculating. Over time column arithmetic became known as *algorism*—the Latin name for al-Khwarismi (Guedj 1996). Today we use the term *algorithm*.

Why Did the Development of Place Value Take So Long?

What makes place value so difficult? Why did it take so long to be developed? For one thing, the idea of zero is conceptually different from all previously developed numbers in that it is not connected to real objects. Piaget noted that the concept of zero introduced number as an idea in itself, separate or abstracted from concrete reality (cited in Guedj 1996). Then, too, the idea of zero evolved in stages. First it was simply functional, a symbol that represented what happened to a number when it was multiplied by ten (324×10 became 3240). Later it was used to stand for the absence of objects in column notation. Only much later in its development did it become a number of its own, defined mathematically as $n - n$ (Guedj 1996).

Children have this same struggle with zero. Recall how Madeline's children figured out that a necklace with 20 beads could be bought with two dimes and no pennies, yet they still thought of 30 and 40 as whole quantities, not as three dimes and no pennies, or four dimes and no pennies. They needed to check out Ellie's conjecture about the zero with other numbers. They did not automatically see that the zero meant no pennies. Children also often write numbers above 100 with two zeroes—using 10013 for one hundred and thirteen, for example. They do not fully understand the combination of the place value columns and the use of zero.

In addition, the idea that a numeral can represent ones or tens or hundreds, depending on where it is placed, involves the big idea of unitizing. The numeral 2 represents two units, but the units themselves can change; they can be ones or tens or hundreds or thousands or more. Cognitively, this is another abstraction from concrete objects. The unit is a variable. Its amount changes depending on the column in which it is placed. The numeral 2 simply represents the cardinality of the units.

Variable

HELPING CHILDREN DEVELOP
MATHEMATICAL NOTATION

Just as these ideas were difficult for humans to invent, evolving only slowly over many, many years, they are huge developmental milestones in the mathematical development of young children. Martin Hughes (1986) showed children between the ages of three and seven several different cans containing different-sized groups of plastic bricks (one, two, three, five, and six) and asked them to put something on paper to show how many bricks were in each of the cans. The developmental progression he found paralleled the historical progression of the development of numerical writing.

Many of the youngest children made idiosyncratic drawings that seemed to have no connection at all to quantity. They just drew pictures of the objects with no attempt to represent the amount. As the big idea of one-to-one correspondence was constructed, children began to represent quantity with pictographic representations—they actually drew the bricks, one for one, to show the amount. Later the representations took on an iconic representation, with slash marks or dots used as *symbols* to represent the quantity of the objects. Eventually, but not without a great deal of struggle, children attempted to represent the quantity with only one symbol. Understanding that one symbol can represent the whole amount requires an understanding of cardinality. This is a landmark leap for children.

A Window into a Classroom

Jodi Weisbart (2000), a K–1 teacher in New York City, set out in the beginning of a school year to investigate how her children would represent quantity. She began by giving the children various bags of objects and asking them to make signs for their bags to show how many objects they had.

Look at the work of Jack and Susie in Figures 4.1a and 4.1b. Both use a pictorial representation. Jack had a bag with seven teddy bears. He drew every bear in the bag, matching their color: four are green, three are red. Susie had a bag with fifteen Unifix cubes: eight yellow, seven red. Like Jack, she drew every cube, matching color and quantity. On the other hand, some of the children used an iconic representation. For example, Ronald had a bag with fourteen teddy bears, but he drew fourteen circles (see Figure 4.2). Interestingly, he still matches the colors. Most of the children, after drawing pictures or representations of what was in their bag, also added numerals. Were they drawing only because they liked to draw? Or did they need to

pictorial vs. iconic representation

FIGURE 4.1a *Jack represents 7 bears pictorially*

represent pictorially what they were beginning to try to represent symbolically? How could Jodi challenge them? What investigation should she plan next?

Historically, it was the need to represent and communicate about larger amounts that led humans to develop numerical symbols. Jodi hypothesized that if she asked her students to represent larger amounts, perhaps they would find the drawing and counting tedious. Maybe they would attempt to represent the amounts with symbols only. She asked the children to make a sign for the door of the classroom so visitors and the principal would know how many children were in the class.

Raquel made a poster with buttons to represent the twenty-eight children—an iconic representation (see Figure 4.3). Because there were so many buttons, however, and now *they* needed to be counted, she wrote counting numerals next to each button. She represented her counting action, but not the cardinality—not the result of the counting. Julie proceeded in a similar fashion but realized that the end result must be represented. "Otherwise vis-

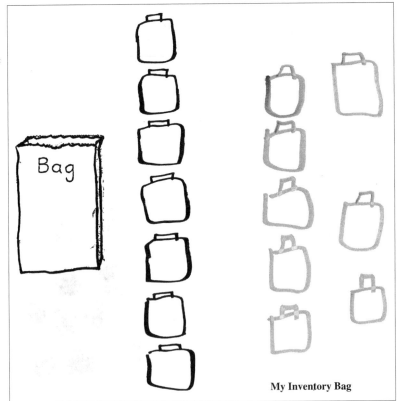

FIGURE 4.1b
*Susie represents 15 cubes
pictorially*

My Inventory Bag

itors would not know which number to look at!" she exclaimed as she wrote *28* at the top of her picture. Eliam decided to draw twenty-eight cubbies to show that there were twenty-eight children (see Figure 4.4). His decision and his drawing show he has constructed an understanding of one-to-one correspondence, but like Raquel he does not represent the result of the counting, only the counting itself. He does, however, count in an organized fashion, top to bottom, left to right. Bryce, on the other hand, used only numerals (see Figure 4.5), writing *28* but also representing the counting. His work is a beautiful example of mathematical development. As children begin to construct a new idea, they often still hang onto the old. As they begin to near a new landmark, we can look back and see evidence of the path they have just traveled.

The large numbers had an even more powerful effect on Ezra, LeeAnne, and Bill. They tired of the counting and attempted to find a way to group the amounts. Here we see the rudimentary beginnings of the use of grouping, rather than counting solely by ones. After several attempts at counting and miscounting, Ezra drew a line across twelve circles and announced, "This is twelve" (see Figure 4.6a). The line was his way of organizing the first twelve into a group so that he didn't have to go back and count them each time.

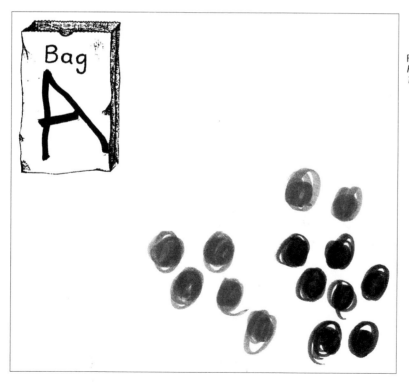

FIGURE 4.2
*Ronald represents
14 teddy bears iconically*

LeeAnne also organized her work (see Figure 4.6b). Her representation is iconic; she used squares to represent the children. But she grouped them by color into sixes as she worked and wrote, "Sics gren [six green], sics red, sics blos [six blues], sics yelos, for prpols [four purples]." When she completed the drawing she wrote 28. Why LeeAnne chose to use sixes is a mystery. And why did Ezra choose twelve? Often as children begin to try to keep track of their work, they choose numbers that are friendly to them. But as they become more comfortable with our number system, their grouping shifts to fives and tens. Bill's work (Figure 4.6c) represents this shift. He also made an iconic representation, but he adds the numerals *10, 10,* and *8* underneath his cubes. In LeeAnne's and Bill's representations we see the beginning of an additive system. Adding the amounts will produce the total quantity.

Working with Context

One way to use context to challenge children is to manipulate the numbers as Jodi did here, by making them larger. Another way is to build in a potentially realized suggestion or constraint. Of course, just because we design

FIGURE 4.3
*Raquel represents
her counting*

a context with suggestions or constraints does not mean our students will experience them as such. Suggestions and constraints themselves must be constructed. Even so, molding the context can be a powerful didactic. To challenge the children to use more grouping, Jodi designed a context with potential grouping suggestions built in. She asked the children to investigate how many cookies would be needed for snack if every child got five and to figure out how many fingers there were in the class of twenty-eight children. For homework she asked them to figure out how many eyes, ears, and fingers there were in their families. In all of these problems children can count by ones if they need to, but the suggestion of grouping (fives, tens, and twos) may lead children to represent the groups.

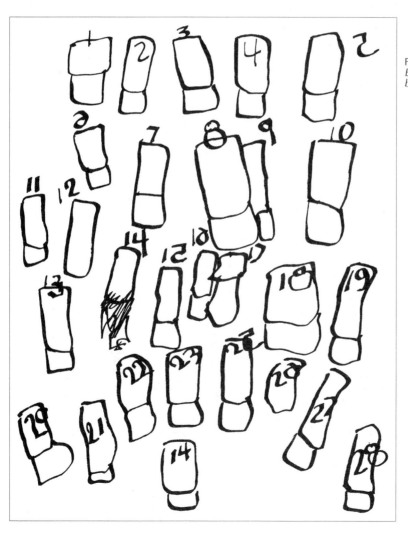

FIGURE 4.4
*Eliam represents 28 kids
by drawing 28 cubbies*

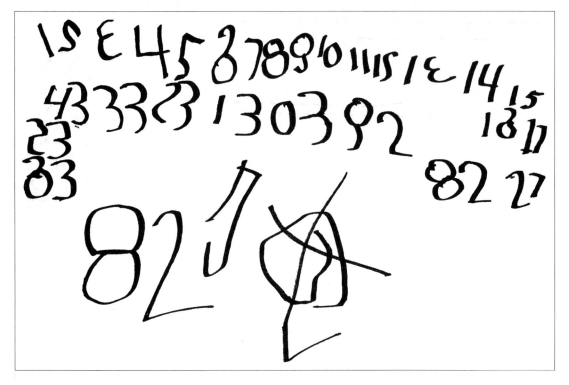

FIGURE 4.5   *Bryce uses numerals only*

FIGURE 4.6a
Ezra draws a line across 12

FIGURE 4.6b   *LeeAnne uses squares in groups of six*

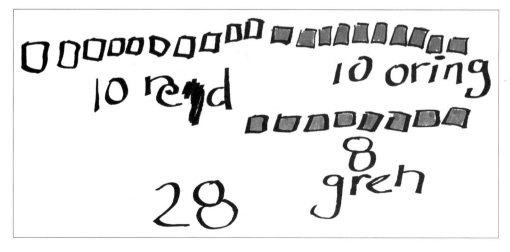

FIGURE 4.6c   *Bill groups by ten*

Ivy did just that (see Figure 4.7). She worked on the snack problem by drawing groups of fives. She put two of these groups together and wrote *10*. She continued like this, drawing every cookie, but symbolizing these groups by skip counting by ten until she reached sixty. Then she probably tired from the tedium of all the drawing, because she shifted her strategy and began to represent the five cookies with only the numeral. And she counted these two fives as ten! Ivy has passed a critical landmark: she is now symbolizing, and grouping two fives to make ten.

For the ears and eyes problem, most children drew ears and eyes, although they did draw *the groups* and then label the amounts. The finger prob-

FIGURE 4.7 *Ivy symbolizes and uses two groups of five to make ten*

lem, however, did result in the shift in representation Jodi was anticipating. For example, Julie used an additive system based on tens: $10 + 10 + 10 = 30$. Martin and Everett drew circles and counted on by ten. Underneath the circles they labeled the number of children. They not only used a symbolic strategy but also used numbers in two ways simultaneously—to represent the fingers and the people! One group of ten (one person) equals ten units (ten fingers).

To support this beginning ability to represent groups of ten symbolically, Jodi next had her students take an inventory of the classroom books. The books used for reading workshop were kept in plastic bins, categorized by author, subject matter, or level. Jodi supplied rubber bands and suggested that the children group the books in each bin into stacks of ten and put a rubber band around each group, and then put a sticky note on each bin indicating how many packs of ten books, how many loose books, and how many books all together (Figure 4.8 shows labels made by Eva and

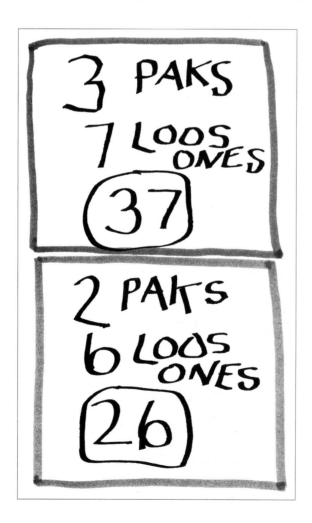

FIGURE 4.8
Eva and LeeAnne make signs for the bins

LeeAnne). By the end of this inventory activity, almost all the children were representing numerically and were discussing the place value pattern that was appearing in their representations.

THE DEVELOPMENT OF ORGANIZATION AND A SYSTEM OF TENS

As illustrated in Chapter 3, counting as a way to understand quantity is not a simple activity for young children. Tagging and synchrony when counting, cardinality, and hierarchical inclusion take a long time to develop. Before they begin to construct these ideas, children see no need to rearrange grouped objects with a clear beginning and end, and thus they often recount the same objects many times. As they begin to see the need for organization as a way to keep track, and as they encounter larger groups of objects, they begin to find ways to organize their counting with landmark numbers such as five or ten.

Kamii (1989) reports how children will often say, "Ten, twenty, thirty," etc. louder as they count, in a sense marking ten but not yet making groups of ten. This idea is, of course, insufficient, because if they lose track of where they are as they are counting, it is still difficult to go back and find the group of ten from which to count on. As we saw with Jodi's students, this dilemma is often the impetus for children to find a way to organize objects into groups as they count. And so we begin to see children get to ten, move those objects into a separate pile, then count to twenty, and again move those objects. To check the amount, they skip count by ten: "Ten, twenty, thirty. . . ." Only much later in their development do they think of making groups first, then counting *the groups* by ones and multiplying that count by ten. This latter strategy is based on the big idea of unitizing, an idea Martin and Everett were beginning to construct.

To construct an understanding of unitizing, children almost have to negate their earlier idea of number. They have just learned that one object needs one word—that *one* means one object, that *ten* means ten objects. Now, ten objects are one—one ten. How can something be simultaneously one and ten?

Let's watch children struggling with this idea in a K–1 classroom in Missouri, toward the end of the school year. For several weeks the children have been packaging T-shirts in quantities of ten for a PTA sale and determining how many ten-packs and how many loose T-shirts they would need to fill various orders (for example an order for eighty-three T-shirts would need eight ten-packs and three loose T-shirts). The classroom teacher, Linda Jones, designed the context to support the development of place value.

Today consultant Cathy Fosnot is visiting the classroom, and she and Linda expand the context to include addition. They present the children with several T-shirt orders (for example, one order is for twenty-nine medium T-shirts and seventeen large T-shirts) and ask them to figure out how many T-shirts in total customers should be billed for.

Amy comes up to the chart where Cathy is sitting holding a marker. She faces her classmates and explains, "I left the twenty-nine alone and I had seven. I counted up to twenty-nine. Then I put seven fingers up, and I counted that, and then I put one more on."

Cathy asks, "When you added the seven to twenty-nine, you used your fingers. Can you do that out loud for us?"

Amy holds up seven fingers, but says, "Thirty, thirty-one, thirty-two, thirty-three, thirty-four, thirty-five, thirty-six . . . thirty-seven."

Cathy draws an open number line (see Figure 4.9a) to represent Amy's thinking and asks, "How do we know when to stop?"

Amy repeats, "I counted up to seven on my fingers."

Cathy draws Amy's attention to the open number line. As Amy uses her fingers once again, Cathy points to each bump of one on the line. They end on thirty-six. "But I have one more to go. I need eight, because there is one more here." She points to the numeral 1 in the 17.

"Is this one?" Cathy asks. "If I do all these seven and one more, will I have done seventeen T-shirts?" Amy tries to explain but gets confused. Cathy attempts to bring the other children into the discussion. "Who can help us? She has done seven so far. How many more does she need to make seventeen?" Several children call out, "Ten"; others begin to count on their fingers from thirty-six.

Megan comes to Amy's aid. Counting on her fingers, she says, "Ten more,

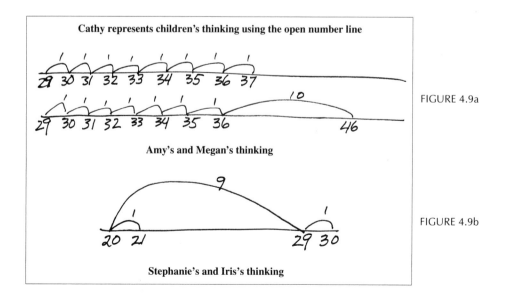

Cathy represents children's thinking using the open number line

FIGURE 4.9a

Amy's and Megan's thinking

FIGURE 4.9b

Stephanie's and Iris's thinking

no nine." They check together, as do several other children, until consensus is reached that ten more are needed.

Cathy draws a leap of ten on the open number line, asking, "So how many T-shirts is that now?" Megan and Amy agree that it is forty-six.

Amy begins by adding seven onto the twenty-nine. But rather than calculating the 1 in the 17 as a ten, she treats it as a one and then gets lost. She does not automatically know that the 1 in 17 is one group of ten. She and Megan must count on, using their fingers, in order to figure it out.

Contrast Amy's understanding with that of Stephanie and Iris as we listen to Stephanie explain how she and Iris figured out an order for twenty-one medium T-shirts and nine extra-large ones: "We knew that twenty-one and nine make thirty because we knew that twenty plus nine was twenty-nine and one more is thirty."

"Oh, so you split the twenty-one up into twenty and one, and started with twenty?" Stephanie nods in agreement. Cathy again uses an open number line to represent their thinking (see Figure 4.9b). "And then, like a big frog jump, you went from twenty right to twenty-nine?"

"Yep, and then we put the one back on, and we knew it was thirty," Stephanie concludes with certainty.

Stephanie flexibly decomposes the twenty-one into 20 + 1. Further, she understands that when the nine is added to twenty, the total automatically becomes twenty-nine. She does not need to count on because she understands the number system—how units are added to the tens.

Joey then explains that his order for twenty-five large T-shirts, twenty-five medium T-shirts, and twenty-five small T-shirts can be solved by calculating 20 + 20 + 20 + 10 + 5. Although all the children understand where Joey has gotten the twenties, there is some confusion over whether 20 + 20 + 20 equals 60. Jennie and Sarah help him explain, using coat hangers packed into groups of tens that Linda has provided as a manipulative during these investigations.

Jennie lays out two piles of ten coat hangers and says, "That's twenty: two-packs, like if you take off the zero." She continues taking a pack of hangers at a time and says, "Thirty, forty, fifty, sixty."

Cathy points to two packs of hangers at a time, "So that's twenty, forty, sixty?"

Sarah completes the explanation. "Yes, see you need six packs of tens . . . one, two, three, four, five, six." Then she recounts by tens, "Ten, twenty, thirty, forty, fifty, sixty."

Here the children are beginning to quantify packs. They talk about two packs being twenty and six packs being sixty. Unitizing is in place—two can represent two loose shirts, or two packs of ten shirts for a total of twenty. A multiplicative system rather than an additive one is being used. A landmark on the landscape of learning has been passed.

INVESTIGATIONS TO FACILITATE PLACE VALUE DEVELOPMENT

Place value involves the big idea of unitizing. Any meaningful context that involves children in packing items into groups and keeping track of loose items is likely to bring the idea of unitizing to the surface for discussion. Teachers find various ways to make such packing contexts their own, ways that are connected to the lives of the children in their classrooms.

Several examples have already been described in this book. Madeline Chang has her students build necklaces by alternating five beads of one color with five beads of another color. They charge one cent per bead and make charts for the cashiers that show how many dimes and how many pennies different-sized necklaces will cost. Linda Jones has her students create ten-packs of T-shirts for the PTA sale and asks them to make a chart that will show how many packs and how many loose T-shirts will be needed to fill various orders. Jodi Weisbart asks her students to take inventory of classroom materials.

One day Lisa Merideth, also a teacher in Missouri, saw the school's secretary counting out handouts for each class. But the phone kept ringing, making her lose track. Lisa and her students came to the rescue: they separated the handouts into stacks of ten and made a chart for the secretary showing how many packs and how many loose sheets she needed for each class in the school.

Naomi Cortez in New York City, developed a context around packing Lifesavers and making a chart for the Lifesaver Company, which is in Port Chester, New York. Joy Whitenack and her colleagues (Whitenack et al. in press) developed a context around Aunt Mary's Candy Store.

One year Susannah Blum, a teacher in New York City's East Harlem, helped her students plant a garden outside the classroom window (Blum 1999). Since the children had been busy ordering seeds, Susannah developed a context around a seed company, Seed Time, that specialized in mailing very expensive, hybrid seeds that got sent in envelopes containing an index card with the seeds taped to it in two groups of fives. Susannah hoped that her children might use the quinary structure to think about two fives making a ten and use this to count seed orders by tens or fives rather than ones. The landscape of learning Susannah anticipated over the course of the investigation is shown in Figure 4.10. Note how it parallels the development of early number systems. She anticipated that many of her children would need to draw each seed to be sure they had twenty-eight, but since the context required figuring out how many envelopes the company should send, she also expected they would draw a circle around groups of ten. She further anticipated that strategies would range from little organization, to laying the seeds out in groups of ten at the start, to representing the fives and tens in the envelopes, to representing twenty-eight with two envelopes and eight loose seeds. These are all examples of additive number systems. The horizon in the distance was for children to employ a multiplicative number system characterized by place value—that they would know at the start that twenty-eight was made up of two sets of ten units and eight single units.

Figure 4.11 shows the work of six children early in this investigation as they figure out an order for sixty-three seeds. Jeanne draws envelopes but they do not include any representation of quantity. Dominique draws the envelopes and attempts the structure, but it is pictorial rather than symbolic and he counts by ones as he draws. He finishes with only fifty-two seeds drawn in three envelopes. It is interesting, though, that as he works, his envelope changes from holding eight and eight to holding ten and ten. Perhaps he is beginning to organize his counting into groups of ten as a way to keep track more easily. Jennie begins drawing seeds in groups of ten, loses sight of the need to group, draws and counts the remainder by ones, and ends up with fifty-three. Marcia, Brian, and Danny, on the

FIGURE 4.10
Susannah's anticipated landscape of learning

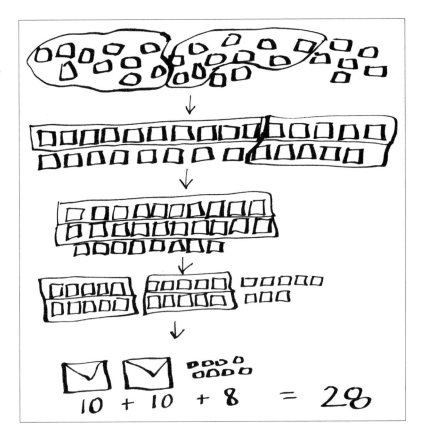

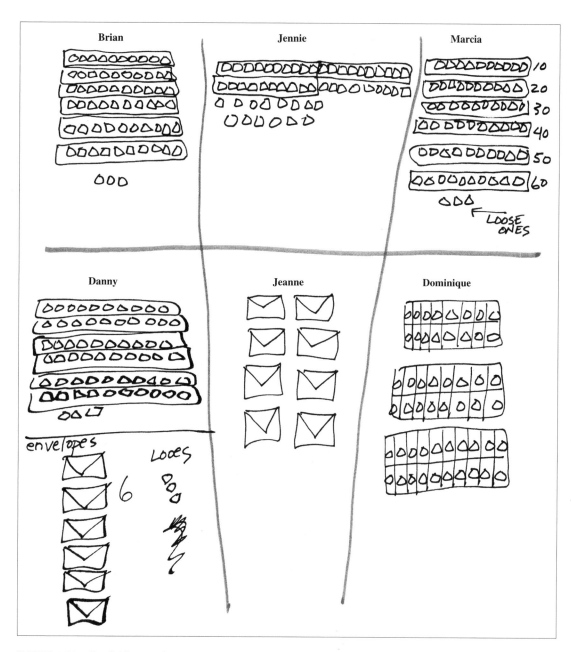

FIGURE 4.11   *Six children's solutions*

other hand, make groups of ten consistently. Marcia keeps track of the quantity as she goes, noting with skip counting (10, 20, 30, and so on). Brian counts the packs when he is done, sure that six packs are sixty. Danny even represents the envelopes and the loose ones using an additive number system.

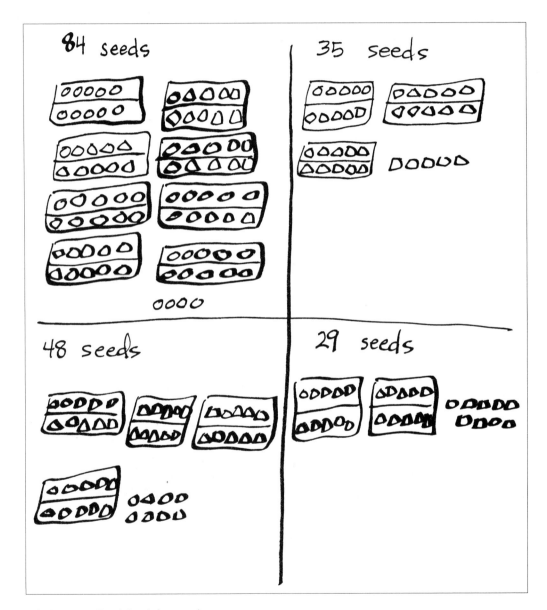

FIGURE 4.12   *Dominique's later work*

As the investigation continued over several weeks, with children packing many different amounts and notating these for the company, strategies began to change. Dominique (see Figure 4.12) is still drawing every seed, but he makes use of the five and ten structure. Jeanne continues drawing envelopes, but she also attempts to keep track of the number of seeds in each (see Figure 4.13). However, this creates a new dilemma for her as she struggles with counting by tens. Note how with 84 she is able to count each envelope by tens; later she becomes confused and reverts to counting by ones as she tries to figure out 48 and 29. Melanie (see Figure 4.14) has clearly understood the ten-seeds-per-envelope structure. And Kenny and Deena

FIGURE 4.13   *Jeanne keeps track of the seeds in the envelopes but struggles with counting by tens*

(see Figures 4.15 and 4.16) construct an additive number system as they work, drawing each seed in the beginning but quickly moving to a system where the envelope represents ten seeds. Note how Kenny has even structured his leftovers into groups of five and how Deena is close to constructing a multiplicative system when she notates with numerals how many of each (envelopes or loose seeds) are needed.

Once children understand unitizing and can anticipate the result of their grouping activities, the horizon shifts and new landmarks appear. They need to explore how many more loose items are needed to get to the next full pack. If children have made charts that show the number of packs and the leftovers, they can add to this chart a third column for the number of loose items needed to make another pack (see Figure 4.17). Note that the numbers in the right two columns add to ten. This idea, that ten must be the result of adding on more loose items to the already loose items if one wants only full packs, will help children when they begin computation with double digits. For example, when adding 38 + 13, an important strategy (see Chapter 8) is to keep the 38 whole, add 2 to get to the landmark number of 40, and then add on 11 more, in leaps of 10 and 1. An alternate strategy is to add on the tens first and then units—for example, 47 + 24 = 47 + 20 + 3 + 1.

FIGURE 4.14
Melanie counts the seeds in the envelopes by tens and then the leftovers by ones

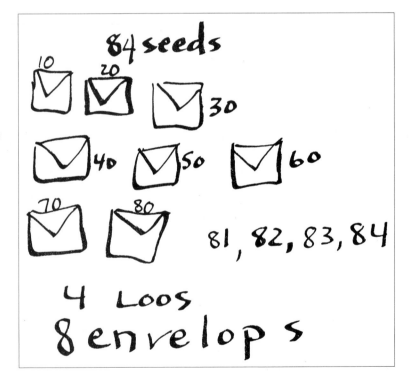

FIGURE 4.15   *Kenny constructs an additive number system*

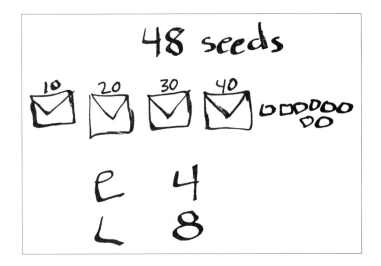

FIGURE 4.16
Deena constructs an additive number system

Children made this chart to help the school secretary know how many packs of paper and loose sheets to give out. The last column shows the number of needed loose ones to make another pack.

Number needed		Packs	Loose	Number needed for another full pack
Fist Grades	63	6	3	7
Sekund	75	7	5	5
3 Third	74	7	4	~~6~~ 4

FIGURE 4.17 *Loose items, packs chart*

SUMMING UP . . .

Developing an understanding of our number system parallels the historical development of number systems. As Hermann Weyl says in the quotation used as an epigraph for this chapter, "Numbers have neither substance, nor meaning, nor qualities. They are nothing but marks, and all that is in them we have put into them by the simple rule of straight succession." Just as human beings put quantitative meaning into symbols over time, children's symbol usage moves from tallies to groups to numerals—from additive systems to multiplicative systems.

Unitizing is the big idea at the heart of place value. Critical addition and subtraction strategies in relation to place value are adding or removing units to get to the next ten (adding 3 to 27 to get to 30 or removing 7 from 27 to get to 20) and adding or subtracting in leaps of ten (16, 26, 36 or the reverse). All of these ideas can be explored in packing contexts like the ones described in this chapter.

As children grapple with these ideas, they construct important mathematical ideas that took centuries to develop. Consider the other epigraph to this chapter: "One is hard-pressed to think of universal customs that man has successfully established on earth. There is one, however, of which he can boast—the universal adoption of the Hindu-Arabic numerals to record numbers. In this we perhaps have man's unique worldwide victory of an idea." When it took humans so long to construct these ideas, how can we not be impressed with the seriousness of young children's mathematical endeavors, their struggles to invent such big ideas, and their capacity to mathematize?

5 | DEVELOPING MATHEMATICAL MODELS

WHAT ARE MATHEMATICAL MODELS?

When mathematics is understood to be mathematizing—the human activity of organizing and interpreting reality mathematically—rather than a closed system of content to be transmitted or even discovered, mathematical models become very important. It is impossible to discuss mathematizing without simultaneously discussing models.

Models are representations of relationships that mathematicians have constructed over time as they have reflected on how one thing can be changed into another and as they have generalized ideas, strategies, and representations across contexts. Although models are used as a lens when new mathematical questions are being explored, they are themselves constructed in the development of our mathematical awareness.

In a sense, models are mental maps used by mathematicians as they organize their activity, solve problems, or explore relationships. For example, when mathematicians are thinking about number, they may have a number line in mind. They think about where numbers are in relation to one another on this line, and they imagine moving back and forth along it. A geometric model of number is another helpful mental map. For example, we might imagine 64 transformed into a square (8×8) and then into a cube ($4 \times 4 \times 4$), and 27 as a smaller cube ($3 \times 3 \times 3$), and then examine how these numbers are related to each other. Some models are based on a network of number relationships based on benchmark numbers, their neighbors, and their use in operations. For example, a mathematician might see the number 64 and immediately think of 2 to the 6th power, or $70 - 6$, or 32 doubled, or 8^2, or $128/2$, or $100 - 36 = 10^2 - 6^2$.

MODELING ACTIONS AND SITUATIONS

When a young child attempts to make lines on a paper to indicate the tree on her street, she begins to model her world. The tree, as she has experienced it, is three-dimensional. She has walked around it, touched the bark, felt the shade from the leaves overhead. The lines she makes on paper are a *representation of* the tree on a two-dimensional plane to communicate to others what she knows a tree to be. The representation is not a copy of what she *sees*; it is a construction, within a medium, of what she *knows*. It is a creation.

Children's early models, in fact, are representations of their interactions with the object, rather than of the object itself. For example, Patrick draws a clock as a series of dots and lines as he says, "Tick-tock, tick-tock." Sara draws a tree as a series of circles because she has run around it. Jay's drawing of his bedroom is a line to represent the path he walks. (See Figures 5.1a–c.) In-

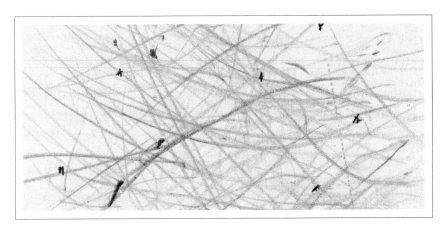

FIGURE 5.1a   *Patrick draws dots and lines to represent the clock*

FIGURE 5.1b
*Sara draws a tree
as circles*

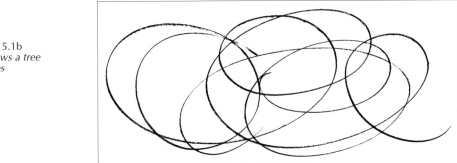

terestingly, children all over the world are likely to draw trees, flowers, or the sun in similar ways. (See Figure 5.2.) Eventually these representations develop into more generalized universal schemas (Kellogg 1969). These generalized models communicate meaning universally and can be used to think with. We have a mental picture of the category *tree,* and a word for it. We can now think about the general idea of a tree without having to recall our actions with regard to a specific tree, and we can use the word to symbolize all trees.

The development of mathematical modeling follows a similar path. When children attempt to model a situation mathematically, they often begin by modeling the actions in the situation. For example, in Chapter 3, when Ginger Hanlon asked her students to figure out whether there would be enough biscuits for everyone, the three children used cubes to model the action of passing out the biscuits. Let's revisit the vignette.

> Yasia suggested using the cubes. "What will you do with the cubes?" I asked.
>
> Yasia, using red cubes, and Dean, using brown, began to put cubes on each of the biscuits on their sheets. Robert decided to give a cube to each child in the classroom, and began to search for orange cubes to hand out.

Dean and Yasia use the cubes in one-to-one correspondence to the biscuits. The cubes are not the biscuits, but they *represent* the biscuits. Although Dean and Yasia can model the situation with the cubes, Robert still needs to act out the situation. He passes out the cubes to the children as if they are the biscuits, without thinking about the total number of biscuits. He models the action, not the situation.

> Dean finished placing his cubes on his biscuits and then began to count them, moving each cube off the biscuit as it was counted. Yasia left the cubes on the biscuits and counted again to 22. She said, "Maybe we'll have three extra." She then noticed that Robert had not finished handing out his cubes. She asked if he had given them to individual children, naming them, and then helped him to

[handwritten marginalia: somewhat similar to tagging?]

[handwritten marginalia: iconic representation but real objects]

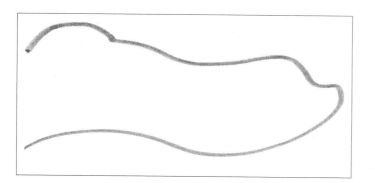

FIGURE 5.1c
Jay's drawing of his bedroom

check that he hadn't forgotten anyone. "Did you give them to the kids in the block area?" she asked. Once satisfied that he had handed out all the cubes, Robert sat down at the table again. Yasia prompted him to go and collect the cubes and count them. Robert did, placing his cubes in a train on the table. He counted them and announced, "Fifteen."

I asked, "Well, now what do we do? Do we have enough biscuits?" Again, Dean immediately said, "Yes, we do. Twenty-two is more than fifteen." Robert looked confused, and I asked him if he knew what Dean meant. He shook his head, and I asked if he knew how he could use the cubes he'd collected and Dean's cubes to figure it out. Again he shook his head, and Yasia, before I could say anything, said, "Robert, you've got the kids and I've got the biscuits. If my train is longer than yours, then we have enough." She took her red cubes off the sheet and put them into a long train. "It's awful

FIGURE 5.2 *Universal schemas in art*

long, isn't it?" she commented. Once she had compared the two trains, she announced that her train of biscuits was longer than Robert's train of kids and so we had enough.

Here the modeling with the cubes resembles two measurement sticks that can be compared. The two trains are laid next to each other, one beside the other. This modeling allows Yasia to compare the two lengths. But now we see her struggle with this comparison model because her hand obscures some of the cubes and she does not maintain the one-to-one correspondence.

> I asked if we had enough left over for the adults. Yasia counted the cubes through the fifteenth one and then, holding the train at that point (but covering some of the cubes as she did so) announced that we had four extra. Dean disagreed, and I asked if there was a way to find out for sure how many extra we had. Yasia immediately began to break up her chain of red cubes (biscuits) and tried to place them on top of each cube in Robert's train of orange cubes (children). I said, "What are you doing, Yasia?"
>
> "I'm putting the biscuits on the children to see if we have any left over." Experiencing difficulty getting them to stay on, she enlisted Robert's help in holding them and said to Dean, "Here, Dean, you have a go." She let him place some of the cubes on top of the train. They kept falling off. Yasia then decided to put her red cubes underneath the train. Again she got Robert to hold one end of the "children" train as she placed the individual cubes underneath it.

Yasia reverts to modeling the action of passing out the cubes because the comparison model with the cubes alone, as measurement sticks, is difficult for her. In this struggle, though, she at least attempts a comparison model of the situation. And this is a remarkable advance from her modeling of a similar situation a week before, when she drew every child with a cube in hand.

As Yasia, Robert, and Dean participate in activities like these, as they are encouraged and supported in mathematizing situations, their models will go beyond representations of their actions and move toward more generalized models of strategies. They will move from models *of* thinking to models *for* thinking (Gravemeijer 1999; 2000). According to Gravemeijer (2000, 9), "The shift from *model of* to *model for* concurs with a shift in the students' thinking, from thinking about the modeled context situation, to a focus on mathematical relations." This is a major landmark in mathematical development.

FACILITATING THE DEVELOPMENT OF MODELS

How Many People Are on the Bus?

How do we, as teachers, facilitate and support the development of models? Let's look in on a lesson in a Dutch classroom. Kris has just told her first-grade class a story about a bus trip. Both to engage them in the story and to ascertain what they understand, she asks them to join in, to tell about what they know about taking buses.

"You have to tell the driver of the bus how far you are going, and then you have to pay him," five-year-old Jan explains.

"No, you give him your card," Anita says.

"What does he do with your card? Does he only look at it?" Kris asks.

"No, he stamps the card," Anita responds and then continues, "and if you go very far, he gives you a lot of stamps."

Some children disagree. "No, he gives you one stamp."

"Yes, and then you sit and wait for the right stop. I got out at the wrong stop," Frans confesses.

"Mother and I take the bus to my grandmother's every Sunday."

The seasoned young bus travelers proudly share their knowledge with their classmates. However, not all the children have traveled by bus, and even those that have are confused by how the public transport system works. The Dutch system is complicated: the further you travel, the more zones you pass through and the more you have to pay. As the children tell their tales, Kris sees to it that an accurate picture of bus travel emerges. Then she takes the conversation to another level.

"You know the small bus at the zoo?" Kris asks. "It makes a lot of stops, and people can hop on and off as they please. This bus is free, you know. You do not have to pay for it. So people take this bus when they want to sit or do not want to walk." Several children say they have ridden this bus, and Kris continues. "The bus is called the *berenboemel*. Recently I spoke with one of the drivers. You know how small the *berenboemel* is . . . only twelve people can fit. There aren't enough seats for more people! This driver told me that he likes to know how many people are on the bus, so that when he comes to each stop he knows how many more people he can allow on. So every time he comes to a stop, he counts the number of people on the bus. But people are always getting upset with him because all this counting takes too much time. I thought maybe we could help him figure out how many people are on the bus at each stop."

Real life situations

Kris knows that children often like to watch people entering and leaving a bus, and that checking the number of passengers can intrigue them. But she has also chosen this context because it is a real situation that has the potential to prompt students to model addition and subtraction. As the children mathematize the situation and discuss the actions of people getting on and off, Kris anticipates they will be able to develop a generalized model that the class can refer to when discussing adding and removing. Children immediately respond to her question with comments and suggestions.

"He can see the people sitting on the bus."

"He sees people stepping on the bus."

"There are too many people on the bus. Sometimes people have to stand. He can count them stepping on and off the bus."

"He can tell when the bus is empty just by looking."

Kris picks up on the suggestion that the bus driver can keep track of when the people get on and off the bus. "Let's play bus," she suggests. She builds a bus by forming a single line of six chairs and holds up a bus driver's cap. "Who will be the bus driver?"

All the children are into the game, and many raise their hand. Kris asks Charlotte to be the first driver. With a big smile, Charlotte comes and sits in the chair designated as the front of the bus. At each stop Kris lets children get on and off the bus. Charlotte takes her job very seriously. She turns the wheel, makes all kind of sounds when using the brakes, and welcomes the people getting on. After a couple of stops Kris asks her how many children are on the bus. Of course, she does not know; too much has happened and she has been focused only on driving the bus.

Kris deliberately does not ask how many children are on the bus after each stop. She is still trying to make the dilemma—the need to keep track with addition and subtraction—come alive. For the children to become invested in solving the bus driver's problem, for them to become involved in mathematizing, they need to take it on as their own.

Charlotte has now experienced the situation, but she has not had to represent, or model, it. Developing a model now becomes Kris's intent. She starts a new bus route with two people in the bus. "Okay, bus driver, start the bus. Hey, see there is your first stop. I see you can brake well. There are three people waiting at this stop." The three people board the bus, and Kris explicitly focuses on the addition. "Driver, how many people do you have in your bus?"

Charlotte is silent for a long time. At last, she looks around, looks at each of her passengers and nods her head five times. "Five," she says.

"I know it," says Cynthia, who is sitting on the bus as one of the passengers.

Kris prompts her to elaborate. "What do you know, Cynthia?"

"I know two and three is five."

"Two and three is five," Kris repeats, then continues to probe. "Can you tell us how that helps us here?"

"Well, you see, there are three people, and uh . . . there are two people on the bus and three people there. You see, that is two and three, and that is five."

Although several children say they agree with Cynthia, several others still need to count. Kris continues the game a while longer. At the next stop, two more people get on the bus. Once again Charlotte has to count all the people on the bus, starting from one; other children use other strategies, such as counting on.

The children enact several more bus routes with different drivers. Although they have experienced the situation of adding and removing people, discussing their strategies and their results, they have still not represented it. Kris arranges the final stop so that there are once again two passengers on the bus and three people getting on, the situation Charlotte faced earlier.

Charlotte recognizes the duplication. "Hey, that's like how my turn started," she exclaims.

"And a lot has happened in between, hasn't it?" Kris says. "Is there a way

we could tell the story of each stop? Show what happened?" Finally she has
succeeded in creating a situation where the children will need to come up
with their own models, or representations, of the situation.

Several children contribute suggestions, the most common being to
write all the names down. A few feel that names are not necessary; they suggest drawing the situation. On a blackboard, Kris keeps track of all the suggestions. She writes the names of the five children down, and she draws a
bus with two passengers on the bus and three people waiting at the bus stop.

Kris and the children are developing a representation of the situation—
a model: a drawing of a bus and a bus stop and numbers representing the
number of people. This model shows the action involved in the situation;
the drawing depicts precisely how many people are on the bus, how many
get off, and how many people are at the bus stop. Kris did not prescribe this
model; she helped the children develop it through discussion within the
community.

Admittedly, Kris takes a strong guiding role in this lesson, and one
might legitimately wonder whether the picture is really a model for *all* the
children. Different groups of children will develop different models; and since
models arise initially as representations of actions and situations, there will
be individual developmental differences. The developmental process, however, is similar. At first children want to write down all the names, staying

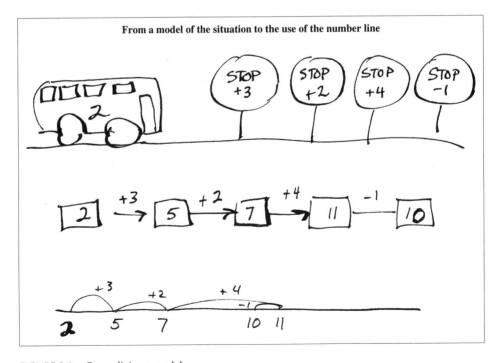

FIGURE 5.3   *Generalizing a model*

close to the real action. Slowly, they start to understand that the names are not important; the bus driver only needs to know how many people are on the bus. (Real bus drivers don't know the names of all their passengers.)

Leaving out the names is usually the first generalization from this specific situation toward a representation for many situations. The first drawings children make often show how many people are on the bus and how many people are waiting to board the bus. Over time, as children examine the situations in which people get on and off the bus, they represent the results of the action with arrows (see Figure 5.3).

Generalizing the Situation, Generalizing the Model

The model Kris's students have developed will help them as they continue to mathematize the problem of the driver of the *berenboemel*. They are developing meaningful symbols to depict addition and subtraction situations. Jan van den Brink (1991), a researcher from the Freudenthal Institute in the Netherlands, developed the bus context. His research shows that the arrows depicting the actions in the bus context help children construct an understanding of the operations of addition and subtraction. He suggests that these arrows can then be generalized to the model of the open number line. An open number line doesn't represent every whole number, only the numbers resulting from the particular action. This more generalized model can be used across many addition and subtraction situations to represent children's strategies (Whitney 1988; Treffers 1991).

The first model Kris's students developed—the list of names—is closely related to the situation they experienced in class. The other models are increasingly more distant from the situation. In the drawing, the names of the children are lost, while the actions—boarding and getting off the bus—are still visible. The arrow model is still a model *of* the situation: all the specifics are imbedded. On the open number line these actions are no longer visible. By helping children generalize the model to all addition and subtraction situations, we facilitate the development of a model *for* many different situations, a model that can eventually be a tool to think with.

One problem with the bus context is that children may conceive of the line as the bus trip itself, in which case a leap back (from 11 to 10, for example) may not be seen as one less person but as a backing-up. Or, children may want to place the 10 to the right of 11, in the sequential position of the trip, but still represent it with a leap of −1 for the person that got off. Another problem is confusion about whether the intervals or the marks denoting the intervals are being counted on a number line. Are the people represented by the intervals (the two units of space between the numbers 5 and 7, for example) or the lines that denote the numbers (in this case, 5, 6, and 7)? Under the latter interpretation, children might argue that three people got on.

Koeno Gravemeijer (1999; 2000) feels that a measurement context, like measuring the height of a can with Unifix cubes and adding or removing units of length, is more closely connected to the leaps and the placement of numbers on the open number line. He suggests the bus context be replaced by a series of measurement activities that develop an understanding of measurement of an iterated unit and only then helping learners to connect the idea of iterated units to the open number line.

A Walk in the City

Jennifer DiBrienza, a first/second-grade teacher in New York City, tried developing a measurement context around the grid pattern of the streets and avenues in Manhattan, where the avenues run north to south, and the streets run east to west. The children are very familiar with this context, because it is so much a part of their lives. They walk up and down avenues, crossing streets along the way. New Yorkers constantly talk about how many blocks they have to walk; it is the way city distances are measured.

Jennifer told her students that over the weekend her friend Shaun, who lives on the corner of 16th Street and 6th Avenue, had decided to walk to Macy's, on the corner of 34th Street and 6th Avenue. When he got there, he wondered how many blocks he had walked. Could they help Shaun find out?

The children set to work. Steve begins by literally drawing the avenue with an arrow and enumerating each street that must be crossed (see Figure 5.4a). Then he counts and writes, "He walked 18 blocks." Breton does not draw the avenue, but she draws each block and labels each street, then counts as well (see Figure 5.4b). Although she wrote the numerals *80*,

FIGURE 5.4a *Steve draws the avenue with an arrow and marks each street that must be crossed*

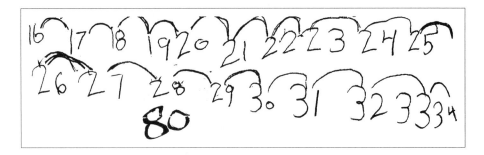

FIGURE 5.4b *Breton draws each block with a jump and labels each street*

she said "Eighteen" as she wrote. Josh also counts, but he labels the blocks as well as the streets (see Figure 5.4c). His work represents a shift from representing the action and then counting the blocks that one walks to using numerals to represent the situation.

With Eve, the development of modeling is even clearer (see Figure 5.5a). She represents the situation in three parts, not in the order of the action but in terms of the relationships she sets up with the numbers. She uses numerals to represent the distance between the numbers. First she declares, "It

FIGURE 5.4c   *Josh counts and labels both the blocks and the streets*

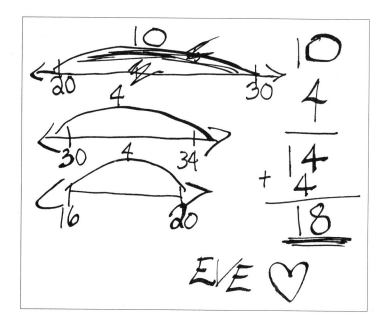

FIGURE 5.5a
Eve represents the situation in three parts, not in the order of the action but in terms of the relations she sets up with the numbers

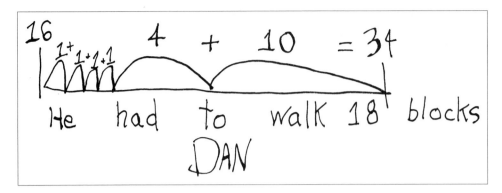

FIGURE 5.5b   *Daniel represents each block between 16th street and 20th street, and then he shifts to representing number relations on a line, taking jumps of 4 and 10*

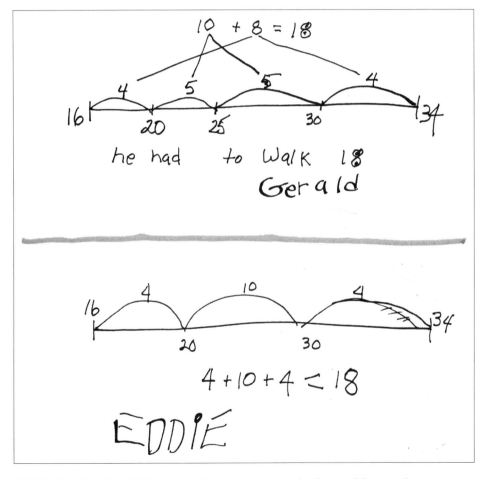

FIGURE 5.6   *Gerald and Eddie show evidence of using a number line model as a tool*

is ten blocks from twenty to thirty." She represents this piece first and then the distance between 30 and 34. Last, she represents the distance from 16 to 20, even though this would have been the first part of the journey. Her model isn't tied to the action at all. This is also the case with Daniel (see Figure 5.5b). He begins by representing each block between 16th Street and 20th Street but then he shifts, like Eve, to representing number relations on a line. He marks leaps of 10 and 4, although a person walking covers only one block at a time. He is beginning to use the number line model as a tool. Gerald and Eddie also use a number line model as a tool to depict the number relationships and to help them calculate (see Figure 5.6). Their models are tools to think with.

THE ROLE OF CONTEXT

The open number line models developed by Jennifer's students evolved out of the street context. However, many children still connect their model to the situation. Will they be able to use the model in other contexts? How do we help children generalize from a particular situation to all subtraction and addition situations? How do we help them generalize the number line model across contexts so that it can be a helpful tool, a model for thinking across contexts—a model to calculate with?

Subtraction Contexts

Daniel, Gerald, and Eddie represented the distance problem with a number line model. But when they were subsequently asked to figure out how much Shaun had spent—he went into the store with $34 in his pocket and only had $16 remaining when he came out—the boys' modeling and strategies changed. In the distance problem they added on; with the money problem they drew 34 tallies to represent the dollars and then removed 16 to represent the money remaining in Shaun's pocket. They counted three times; first the 34 tallies, then the 16 they removed, and then the remaining 18. Why would they shift their strategies?

The distance problem has a part/whole context (the 16 is inside the 34) and the action in the situation (physically advancing from 16 to 34) suggests an adding on strategy. In contrast, the money problem, while it also has a part/whole context—the $16 is part of the $34—suggests an image of 34 as a whole, with something being removed.

Let's consider a few more subtraction contexts. The problem *Jasmine is 12 and her mom is 43. How much older than Jasmine is her mom?* is not a part/whole situation. It is more likely to be modeled as comparison and counting on. On the other hand, *Jasmine's mom had made 43 cupcakes. She brought a dozen to the bake sale. How many did she have left for Jasmine and her family to eat?* is more likely to be modeled as a removal. Packaging contexts like those described in Chapter 4 are likely to be modeled by grouping. For example: *Our class needs more magic markers because they are starting to dry out. We would like to have 70 good markers in the classroom. Steve has lots of*

markers in the supply room. They come in packs of 10. We have 2 boxes of 10 mark-
ers and 3 single markers that still work. How many markers do we have to get
from Steve to have 70? Many children will model the problem with groups of
tens, adding on seven markers first and then four boxes, or adding boxes
first and then single markers.

Of course, models cannot be transmitted any more than strategies or
big ideas can be transmitted; learners must construct them. Just because we
plan a context with a certain model in mind does not mean that all learners
will interpret, or assimilate, the context that way. But it is *likely* that a particular context will affect the children's modeling and strategies in a particular way, and it is on that basis that we design our curriculum. The bus and
city walk scenarios are examples of dynamic situations in which a change
occurs that can be captured in arrow models, which can then be generalized
to an open number line. The open number line can eventually be used to
represent the addition and subtraction.

CONNECTING ADDITION AND SUBTRACTION; CONNECTING THE MODELS

Do subtraction and addition need different contexts? In the bus context, addition and subtraction were intermingled: getting on and off the bus go well
together. In Jennifer's class, many of the children solved the subtraction problems with an addition, or adding on, strategy.

That subtraction and addition are related is a big idea children need to
develop. Eventually it is important that children know that either strategy
can be used. For example, if the distance problem had been *Jason lives on
East 2nd Street and walked up First Avenue to East 34th Street,* adding on would
not be very efficient, because 2 is so far away from 34. It would be much
more efficient to remove 2 from 34, but the context is more likely to be modeled with counting on.

Children need to understand the connection between addition and subtraction. Further, they need to understand that comparison and removal contexts both can involve subtraction. Traditionally, teachers have often told
learners that subtraction means "take away." This is a superficial, trivialized
notion of subtraction, if not erroneous. It is just as erroneous to say subtraction means "difference." Subtraction is a *generalized* notion of the connection
between the models, between the actions of removal and difference. And
this big idea must be constructed by learners.

In a keynote address at the Exxon Educational Foundation Conference
in 1999, Glenda Lappan told about an experience she had had as a teacher.
After completing an achievement test, one of her students came up to her
and said, "Did you see, the baseball problem was on the test?"

"Well," Glenda said, "I had seen the test and there was no baseball problem on it. So I asked the girl what she meant. The answer was very informative. This student had recognized that one of the problems on the test could

be solved the same way we had solved a problem in class earlier. The class problem had been about baseball. But the test item was not."

This generalizing across problems, across models, and across operations is at the heart of models that are tools for thinking. Models *for* thinking are based on the development of number relationships. This includes operations. To have a general model in mind when mathematizing, one has to understand the connection between the operations (e.g, addition and subtraction) and one has to have a generalized notion of each of the operations that is not bound to the context.

How do we develop this generalizing? Jennifer DiBrienza purposely asked her students to solve two related problems about her friend Shaun. She knew the distance problem was likely to generate, at least for some children, adding-on strategies. The money problem had the potential to generate removal strategies. She kept the numbers the same, however, hoping children who solved them differently might be intrigued enough to explore the connections.

Several children noticed the connection between the two problems. In Raquel's words, "It is almost the same only backwards, so I knew the answer right away." For others, the connection was not clear. Steve made the same drawing for both situations and never realized the connection until math congress, when Raquel pointed it out to him. Theo did not see the connection either; he saw two different problems and used two different approaches (see Figure 5.7). Theo's modeling of the second problem is interesting. He was puzzled by it, and a classmate suggested he use a number line picture as he had with the first problem. But because he is removing in the second problem, he places the numbers in descending order: from 34 to 30 to 20 to 16. The model is still a representation of the situation. He has not yet generalized how the actions of subtraction and addition are reversed on the number line. He could see the same model in both problems, but he had to adapt it to represent his thinking. Clearly, he started with 34 and worked backward. For him the question was how many "jumps" are there between 34 and 16. He put the 34 on the left and worked to the right, toward 16.

Juxtaposing contexts that have the potential to generate different models and strategies but keeping the numbers the same is one way to encourage children to explore relationships and to generalize. Another is to play with the numbers in the problems. For example, consider the following contexts related to books.

> Ms. DiBrienza LOVES to read! She is always reading lots of different books and magazines. Right now, she is reading a novel with a friend, Ginny, and she is reading another book on her own. Can you help her solve these problems?
>
> The book she is reading with Ginny has 107 pages. Ms. DiBrienza is on page 64. How many more pages does she need to read to finish the book?
>
> Ginny is reading the same book, but she is only on page 43. How many more pages does Ginny need to read to finish the book?

Ms. DiBrienza is also reading a book about math. It has 203 pages. She is on page 18. How many more pages does she have to read in this book?

Jennifer chose the numbers in the problems on purpose. She anticipated that most children would not immediately see the connection between the first and the second situation. After all, to fully understand the connection between the problems, the children have to understand the connection between addition and subtraction. They have to understand the relationship between the part—the number of pages read already—and the whole—the number of pages the book contains. Although children may not connect

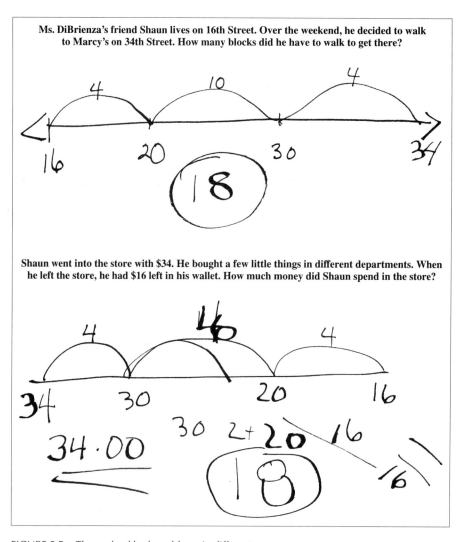

FIGURE 5.7   *Theo solved both problems in different ways*

these problems as they work, Jennifer anticipates she may be able to trigger a wonderful, rich conversation during the subsequent math congress. With the third situation, the math book, Jennifer anticipates that because 18 is so far away from 203, some children may find it tedious, or cumbersome, to add on. If they explored the related addition and subtraction in the first two problems, they might consider a removal strategy in the math book problem, even though the problem is more likely to suggest the use of adding on.

Because this series of problems was given to the children late in the year when much work had already been done with the open number line model, many of the children used it as a tool. For the first problem, Eve makes a jump from 64 to 70, then a jump of 30 to the benchmark number of 100, then a final jump of 7 (see Figure 5.8a). Erica makes smaller jumps (see Figure 5.8b): she uses the tens as friendly numbers; one jump of 30 is still too much for her. Lucy and Mercy (see Figure 5.8c) search for even more support: instead of a first jump of 6 they make six jumps of 1. Although all of these children

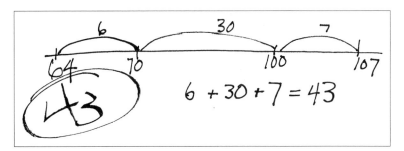

FIGURE 5.8a
Eve uses benchmark numbers

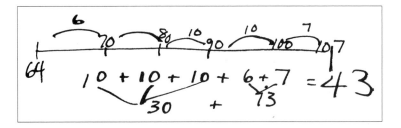

FIGURE 5.8b
Erica makes smaller jumps, using the tens as friendly numbers

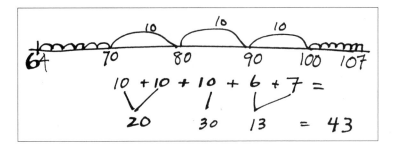

FIGURE 5.8c
Lucy and Mercy use six jumps of 1 to go from 64 to 70

use the open number line to represent their strategies, they do not model the relationships between the problems.

Frederick, on the other hand, constructs the relationship as he works. He begins by representing each situation on the open number line, but as he works he suddenly connects the problems, stops working, and writes, "same." Jennifer's strategy of juxtaposing the contexts has succeeded in helping him generalize. Daniel's and Ari's work (see Figure 5.9) also shows evidence of an understanding of the relationships, although it is not clear whether they constructed this understanding as they worked or whether they knew it already.

Devising rich contexts and playing with the numbers in the problems will not by themselves cause children to generalize. Many children in Jennifer's class do not construct relationships between the problems, even

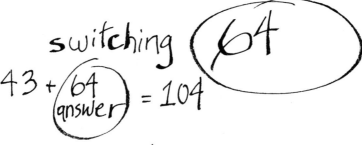

FIGURE 5.9   *Ari and Daniel see the relation between the two problems*

though she has juxtaposed the contexts and numbers, and even though she will have a math congress on these ideas. As adults, with better mathematical understanding, we immediately see the models in the problems and we expect that the children should. But it is important to realize that the models are not in the problems until we mathematize them as such. Children who have not constructed the relationships will mathematize the situations in relation to *their* insights, *their* strategies, *their* ideas. But juxtaposing contexts and playing with the numbers in them may invite some children to reflect on the relationships. At a minimum, Jennifer is likely to be able to have a "juicy," rich conversation on these relationships during her math congress.

SUMMING UP . . .

It is impossible to talk about mathematizing without talking about modeling. Mathematical models are mental maps of relationships that can be used as tools when solving problems. These pictures, or mental maps, are powerful ways to help us understand and represent our world.

Models themselves are constructed. They emerge from representations of the *action* in the situation. For example, children don't represent a tree as an object; they represent their actions in relation to the tree. Later these representations of action develop into representations of the situation using cubes or drawings. Eventually, modeling develops into a symbolic representation of mathematizing. Children represent the *strategies* they used to solve the problem, rather than the situation. For example, children may represent a walk in the city in leaps of tens, even though the distance is actually covered one block at a time. Or they may represent the pieces of the walk in a different sequence, one that represents their calculation strategy rather than the sequence in which the walk happened. As teachers work with children with models such as the open number line, these representations of their strategies develop into mathematical models of number relationships; they develop into *mathematical tools*.

The developmental process is characterized by generalization. The importance of generalization in learning cannot be overstated. Piaget (1977) called it "reflective abstraction" and argued that it was the driving force in learning. The mathematician Jacobi, describing his own mathematical thinking process, said, "One should always generalize." Each developmental shift produces a different way of symbolizing. The model eventually must be able to signify the relationships between numbers and between operations.

At the heart of modeling is number sense—the representation of number relationships. As children construct mental maps of these relationships, they are developing powerful tools with which to continue to mathematize their own lived worlds. As Samuel Karlin states so well in one of the epigraphs to this chapter, "The purpose of models is not to fit the data but to sharpen the questions."

6 | ADDITION AND SUBTRACTION FACTS ON THE HORIZON

"Can you do addition?" the White Queen asked.
"What's one and one and one and one and one and
one and one and one and one and one?"
"I don't know," said Alice. "I lost count."

—*Lewis Carroll*, Through the Looking Glass

We used to think that if we knew one, we knew two,
because one and one are two. We are finding that we
must learn a great deal more about "and."

—*Sir Arthur Eddington, quoted in* Mathematical Maxims
and Minims

TEACHING BASIC FACTS

To Memorize, or Not to Memorize?

To really understand addition and subtraction, we must understand how they are connected. We must also have a generalized model of the operations, one that can be used as a tool to think with no matter what the context (e.g., understanding how removal and comparison contexts can both be solved by subtraction on a number line). By modeling addition and subtraction situations and then generalizing across these situations, children are able to understand and represent the operations of addition and subtraction.

Once children have constructed these landmarks, the traditional emphasis has been to have them memorize the basic addition and subtraction facts (through 20) through repetitive drill and practice, using worksheets and flash cards. Do these instructional strategies work? Is it necessary to memorize facts? If so, how do we help children journey toward this horizon?

The debate in our schools has commonly centered on understanding vs. memorization, as if the approaches were dichotomies. Students have been left with counting on their fingers on the one hand or memorizing isolated facts on the other. Understanding what it means to add and subtract is necessary before facts can become automatic, but understanding does not necessarily transfer to automaticity. In other words, understanding is necessary but not sufficient. Children often develop a good understanding of what it means to add two numbers, and they demonstrate this understanding by showing with their fingers, or with cubes, the numbers they are adding. Even with this understanding however, they count three times—each quantity separately, then the total. For example, to figure out 5 + 6, they may initially count from one to five, then one to six, and then combine the sets and start all over from one again to count the whole to eleven. Even when they construct the strategy of counting on from the largest number, they may still rely on counting with their fingers, saying, "Seven, eight, nine, ten, eleven."

While these strategies may be wonderful beginnings, children cannot be left with only these ways to solve addition and subtraction problems. But is the answer memorization of isolated facts? How many facts are there? And how do we help children understand the relationships between facts (e.g., 5 + 6 = 5 + 5 + 1)?

Common Addition Strategies

Children who struggle to commit basic facts to memory often believe that there are "hundreds" to be memorized because they have little or no understanding of the relationships among them. Children who commit the facts to memory easily are able to do so because they have constructed relationships among them and between addition and subtraction in general, and they use these relationships as shortcuts. The strategies children most commonly invent and use are:

1. Double plus or minus—for example, 6 + 7 = 6 + 6 + 1 (or 7 + 7 − 1) = 13.
2. Working with the structure of five—for example, 6 + 7 = 5 + 1 + 5 + 2 = 10 + 3 = 13.
3. Making tens—for example, 9 + 7 = 10 + 6 = 16.
4. Using compensation—for example, 6 + 8 = 7 + 7 = 14.
5. Using known facts—for example, 6 + 8 = 14, so 7 + 8 must be 14 + 1 = 15

Memorizing facts with flashcards or through drill and practice on worksheets will not develop these relationships.

Memorization or Automaticity?

Memorization of basic facts usually refers to committing the results of unrelated operations to memory so that thinking is unnecessary. Isolated additions and subtractions are practiced one after another as if there were no relationships among them; the emphasis is on recalling the answers. Teaching facts for automaticity, in contrast, relies on thinking. Answers to facts must be automatic, produced in only a few seconds; counting is not sufficient. But thinking about the relationships among the facts is critical. A child who thinks of 9 + 6 as 10 + 5 produces the answer of 15 quickly, but thinking, not memorization, is at the core (although over time these facts are eventually remembered). The issue here is not whether facts should eventually be memorized but how this memorization is achieved: by drill, practice, and memorization, or by focusing on relationships?

Isn't memorization faster? Interestingly, no! Kamii (1994) compared two first-grade classrooms in the same school. In one the teacher focused on relationships and worked toward automaticity. In the other students memorized facts with the help of drill sheets and flashcards. The children in the classroom in which automaticity was the goal significantly outperformed the traditionally taught students in being able to produce correct answers to basic addition facts within three seconds—76 percent compared with 55 percent. Some of the most difficult facts for the traditional students were 8 + 6, 5 + 7, 5 + 8, 9 + 5, and 7 + 6. These, of course, were solved easily by the other group with strategies like double plus or minus, working with the structure of fives, and making tens.

When relationships are the focus, there are far fewer facts to remember, and big ideas like compensation, hierarchical inclusion, and part/whole relationships come into play. Also, if a child forgets an answer, she has a quick way to come up with it.

FOCUSING ON RELATIONSHIPS

Doubles

Doubles (4 + 4, 5 + 5, 6 + 6, etc.) are important because they are the basis of many of the other facts. Let's listen in as Madeline Chang and her K–1 students investigate doubles. Madeline begins this math workshop by reading the classic children's book *Madeline*, by Ludwig Bemelmans (1977): "In an old house in Paris, that was covered with vines, lived twelve little girls in two straight lines. . . ." Graham, a kindergartner, exclaims, "Hey! They walk in line just like we do!"

Madeline acknowledges his connection and asks, "How many are in each line when they walk?" The children look at the picture and count six. Madeline then asks the children to think about other scenarios—what if there are seven in each line, or eight, or fifteen? How many children will there be then? What about the students in their class—can they all walk in line and each have a partner?

Children set out with drawing paper and markers. Many draw the children in one line first and then complete the second line, counting by ones to get a total. But others draw two children holding hands and count by twos as they work. One of these children, Sadie, works out seven, counting by twos until she reaches fourteen. Then, noticing the pair relationship she exclaims, "Hey, I've got a shortcut. I know seven in each line is fourteen, so if it's eight in each line then it's only two more . . . that's sixteen!"

Sadie's shortcut contains a very important big idea—*when doubling a number, you can count by twos* (i.e., two sevens are equivalent to seven twos). This idea is an important idea in mathematics. It underlies the relationship between odd and even numbers, and it is an example of the commutative property of multiplication. It is also an important step in Sadie's mathematical development. Skip counting by twos is a different strategy for counting. Many of the children in the class are still counting by ones. Madeline recognizes this idea as an important landmark and therefore wants her community of learners to consider it. When she convenes the children for a math congress to discuss their strategies and ideas, she asks Sadie to share her strategy for eight children each of whom has a partner.

"I counted by twos," Sadie announces proudly. She shows her drawing of fourteen children in two lines, holding hands. "See," she continues, "two, four, six, eight, ten, twelve, fourteen. Seven kids in a line. And then I knew it would just be two more."

"Oh, that's cool . . . so it's sixteen for eight," Roland says, acknowledging Sadie's idea and completing the explanation.

Madeline knows that although the children who are already counting by twos can probably follow Sadie's reasoning, those who are still counting one by one may not. She wants to model Sadie's idea—to represent it in a way that will give other children a chance to reflect on it. She decides to use a number line model (see Figure 6.1). She takes a long strip of paper (like a ribbon) and tapes it under the chalkboard, across the whole front of the classroom. On an index card she writes *7 + 7,* tapes it above the strip of paper at the point she has written *14,* and asks Sadie to tape her picture underneath. Next she writes *8 + 8* on an index card, writes *16* on the strip after *14,* and tapes the *8 + 8* index card above *16.* As children share the scenarios they have investigated, they discuss where each one goes on the number line and tape their picture underneath.

Over the next several days, the children explore many different-sized groups (including much larger numbers), and they continue to fill in the number line. Above the line, index cards show the addition (1 + 1, 2 + 2, 3 + 3, etc.). Below, on the paper strip, are the even numbers (2, 4, 6, 8, etc.).

FIGURE 6.1 *Doubles number line*

In between the lines, are their pictures. (Madeline left this "number line" up all year, and the children often referred to it, adding to it while playing a game or when doing mental math.)

As part of their investigation, the children also consider what else comes in pairs, like mittens and shoes. Madeline reads *Shoes, Shoes, Shoes* (1995), by Ann Morris, and tells the children that in her family they all had to take their shoes off at the door. Children draw their own families and figure out how many shoes there will be at the door. The connection between 7×2 and 2×7 is explored further.

"How many shoes for the people in your family, Leroy?" Madeline asks.

"There's seven people in my family, so there are seven pairs of shoes," he announces with assurance, "and that is seven left shoes and seven right shoes, and I know that seven plus seven is fourteen."

Brianna, a kindergartner, wants to draw and cut out her own shoes. So the next day, Madeline suggests they all do this, and the students make a class graph showing the boys' shoes and the girls' shoes. Madeline also makes reduced photocopies of their pictures of their shoes, which she incorporates into a board game she calls Double Your Number (see Figure 6.2). To play,

Madeline's Double Your Number board game

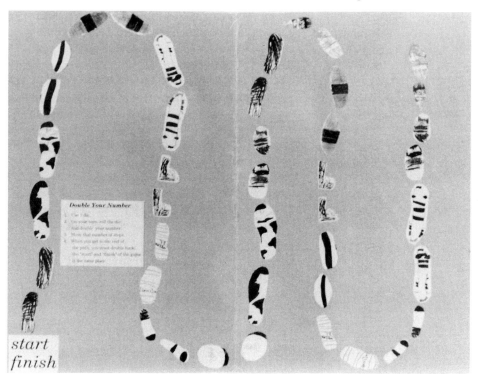

FIGURE 6.2   *Double Your Number*

a die is thrown and the amount on the die is doubled as players move along the board. The idea is to give children an opportunity to experience again and again the doubling of the numbers 1 through 6.

While playing this game, several children who have not yet constructed the logic that Leroy verbalized earlier become very excited over their discovery that the number on the die matches the number of *pairs* of shoes while the doubled total matches the *number* of shoes! Two children in particular, Micky and Ken, find this phenomenon magical and remain puzzled by it for a long time. Finally Micky, with much excitement, figures it out.

"Oh wow . . . I know, Ken. Look," Micky exclaims. "I know why this is happening! There's right shoes and left shoes! When we roll five we get to move ten. But that's five right shoes and five left shoes! But see . . . that's five pairs! It's one of each."

Ken smiles broadly, glad that they have "cracked" the problem. "Oh yeah, like if we get a four, we move eight shoes . . . but that's four pairs. Four left shoes, and four right shoes!"

Although Micky and Ken heard Leroy's and Sadie's explanations a few days earlier and had taken part in the construction of the number line, they had still not constructed the idea that when doubling numbers, you can count by twos that many times. So often we think that because one child has explained an idea to others or because we have done an activity, everyone understands. Micky and Ken are important reminders that learners need to make sense of ideas themselves. The landscape of learning has many paths; construction, not activity or transmission, characterizes the journey.

Combinations That Make Tens

Knowing the combinations that make ten is critical if we want children to be able to solve problems like 7 + 4 by making a ten (7 + 3) and then adding one. Otherwise they will just count on from seven using their fingers. The following investigation, which is very similar to one introduced in Chapter 3, is typical of ones that can be used to focus discussion on the relationships in the combinations that make ten:

> When I was walking to school this morning, I stopped at the grocer on the corner to buy some apples. There were so many kinds, green Granny Smith, red Macintosh, yellow Delicious. They were each packaged ten to a pack, with cellophane over them. I wanted a selection of green Granny Smiths and red Macintoshes, but I didn't want to buy two whole packs. That would be twenty apples! I wasn't that hungry!
>
> I asked the grocer why he didn't make a pack of ten with some red and some green. He said there are so many ways to make them, like one green and nine reds, or five reds and five greens, and so on, that he got confused trying to think of all the ways and had just made all the packs the same! I started wondering, too. How many ways could he make ten-packs containing Macintosh and Granny Smith apples? I told him that I taught a K–1 class in the school down

the road and that we would be happy to investigate all the ways and draw up some plans for him. Can we help him? How many ways are there?

As Chapter 3 explains, a structure is built into this context that is likely to bring up the big ideas of *part/whole relationships* and *compensation*—ideas that underlie the knowledge of all combinations that make ten and the subsequent strategy of making tens for addition. As children set out to make plans for the grocer by investigating all the combinations, many may begin to see that as one Granny Smith apple is gained, one Macintosh is lost. Subsequently, a math congress can be structured around this important landmark by asking, "Did anybody find a way to make a box with only one Granny Smith?" On large graph paper, one green square and nine reds can be colored to match the child's response and then children can be asked, "Did anyone find a way with two Granny Smiths?" As all the combinations that make ten surface, and the documentation on the graph paper grows, the staircase that evolves will surprise and delight students.

Of course, one investigation is probably not sufficient: other contexts need to be designed to continue this journey. Many games can be modified to expose children to combinations that make ten. One is the familiar game of Concentration. Forty cards (a standard deck without face cards) can be placed face down in four rows of ten. Children can take turns turning over two cards at a time, trying to find two cards that will add up to ten. Go Fish, another common childhood card game, can be modified to make the goal combinations that add up to ten. Each player holds five cards in his hand, with the remainder of the deck in a "fish pile" in the center of the playing area. Players take turns asking one another for a card that when combined with a card they are holding will make ten. Completed combinations that make ten are placed in front of each player face up so everyone can check. Dominoes can also be played for combinations that make ten rather than for matches.

USING MANIPULATIVES

In the United States, the manipulatives most commonly used with young children are single objects that can be counted—Unifix cubes, bottle caps, chips, or buttons. While these manipulatives have great benefits in the very early stages of counting and modeling problems, they do little to support the development of the important strategies needed for automaticity. In fact, at a certain point they begin to *reinforce* low-level counting strategies. For example, to solve $6 + 7$ with Unifix cubes, children need to count out six, then seven, and then either "count on" as they combine or (as is most common) count three times—first the two sets, then the total. Because the materials have no built-in structure, they offer little support for the development of alternative strategies.

Building structure into manipulatives is not always beneficial by itself, however. For example, an abacus, Cuisenaire rods, Stern materials, and

Diennes base ten blocks all have a base ten structure built in. The problem with these materials is that while the structures in them are apparent to adults, they are not always apparent to children. Resnick and Omanson (1987, cited in Gravemeijer 1991) give a beautiful example of children's difficulties when using base ten materials:

> A student is looking at six flats (worth 600) and five sticks (worth 50). The teacher asks, "So how much do you think this would be?"
>
> The student answers, touching the hundreds blocks, "100, 200, 300, 400, 500, 600 . . . (touching the tens blocks) 700, 800, 900, ten hundred, eleven hundred."
>
> The teacher asks, "Are these (tens) worth 100?"
>
> "I count them all together."
>
> "But these (tens) aren't hundreds."
>
> "I am counting these like tens," explains the student.
>
> "OK. But how much would these (tens) be worth?"
>
> "Oh. 10, 20, 30, 40, 50. . . . 50 dollars."
>
> So now the teacher asks about the whole amount, "How much would this (entire display) be worth altogether?"
>
> "600 . . . wait! It's 5 and 6."
>
> "But how much is it altogether? This (hundred) is 6, right?"
>
> "Eleven hundred."

If a child has not constructed the big idea of unitizing, she does not see the rod as one ten; she sees it simply as a unit. Similarly, a child placing a blue Cuisenaire rod next to a light green rod does not necessarily think about the quantities they represent; she may be thinking only about the colors.

Cobb (1987) writes:

> the lack of an appropriate explanatory construct to account for the transition from concrete to abstract, conceptual knowledge such as an objectified part-whole structure, is apparent. In lieu of an explanation, it is implied that students *will come to see* various abstract, arithmetical relationships. (18)

As Cobb makes apparent, the learning theory behind the use of these materials is an "activity" or "empiricist" one. The assumption is that if children just use the materials enough, they will "take in," or "come to see," the arithmetical structure. From a constructivist perspective on learning, we need to ask what it is the child is seeing. Holt (cited in Gravemeijer 1991) puts it well:

> The trouble with this theory was that Bill and I already knew that the world of numbers worked. We could say, "Oh, the rods behave just the way numbers do." But if we hadn't known how

number behaved, would looking at the rods have enabled us to find out? (66)

The materials cannot transmit knowledge; the learner must construct the relationships (Gravemeijer 1991).

Streefland (1988) suggests that instead of building adults' mathematical structures into materials, designers look to children's invented alternative strategies as "road signs" and build manipulatives that enable children to realize their own ideas. In this way, structured materials can both support natural development and "stretch" children to restructure an initial strategy and adopt a better shortcut.

The Rekenrek

With these goals in mind—supporting and stretching children's natural development—Adrian Treffers, a mathematics curriculum researcher at the Freudenthal Institute in Holland, developed a tool called the *rekenrek*. Directly translated, *rekenrek* means calculating frame, or arithmetic rack. He also designed an accompanying didactic for using it to support the natural mathematical development of children—to encourage children to use strategies like double plus or minus, working with the structure of five, using compensation, and making tens, and to stretch children toward using these strategies *in place of* counting.

While the *rekenrek* may seem like an abacus at first glance, it is not based on place value columns and it is not used in that way. Rather, it comprises beads in two rows of tens, each broken into two sets of five (see Figure 6.3a). Beads are grouped on the left to represent the amounts being calculated. The five structure offers visual support (the quantity of five can often be subitized as a whole) and supports the discovery that seven comprises five and two; eight, five and three, and so on. Figure 6.3b shows an arithmetic rack with 6 + 7 represented. Children might calculate the total as 6 + 6 + 1, or as 5 + 5 +1 + 2, or as 10 + 3. They can also count three times, or count on, if they need to, but the manipulative is likely to stretch children to structure

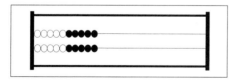

FIGURE 6.3a
The rekenrek

FIGURE 6.3b
6 + 7 on the rekenrek

shortcuts. The arithmetic rack also allows for various strategies with subtraction. Figure 6.3c shows three different ways the rack might be used to solve 13 − 7.

Minilessons Using the **Rekenrek**

We're back in Linda Jones's K–1 classroom in Missouri. Linda has grouped her students around her in the meeting area for a minilesson at the start of math workshop. She is working with a large-scale *rekenrek*. Covering the rack with a piece of fabric so that the children cannot see what she is doing, she moves over to the left six beads on the top and five beads on the bottom. When she finishes, she removes the fabric briefly for all to get a glimpse, but then covers the rack again in order to discourage counting strategies.

Linda invites the children to share what they saw and how they figured out the total. "What did you see? Turn to your neighbor and tell what you did." After a few moments of these paired discussions, Linda starts a whole-group discussion. "Kenny, what did you see?"

"I saw five [red] on the top and one white, and five [red] on the bottom," Kenny replies quickly. But he gets confused trying to explain how many that is and comes up to the now uncovered rack and counts the beads from one to eleven.

His classmate Mike agrees with him but explains that he went, "Seven, eight, nine, ten, eleven."

"Jessie, how about you?" Linda asks. "You had your hand up quickly. What did you do?"

"I didn't have to count," Jessie reports proudly, "because I knew there were five [red] on the top and five [red] on the bottom and that made ten, and one more is eleven."

"Wow, that's a great strategy, isn't it? Maybe some of you might want to try Jessie's strategy on this next one."

FIGURE 6.3c
Various solutions to
13 − 7

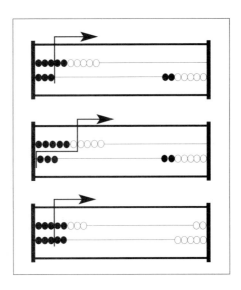

It's not important that everyone share a strategy. Linda elicits three different ones, highlights the efficiency of Jessie's, suggests that others may want to try it, and moves on. She covers the rack up and makes seven and seven behind the fabric. "Okay, here we go." She uncovers the fabric for a quick glimpse. "What do you see? Talk to your neighbor."

"What did you see on the bottom, Andy?"

"I saw five reds and two whites, and I knew that was seven," Andy explains. Jake, who is sitting next to him, interrupts excitedly. "Yup, and on the top, too. Seven and seven."

"And how much is all of that, Jake?" Linda asks.

"Fourteen," Jake says confidently. He continues explaining his thinking. "I took the whites away on the top and the bottom. That gave me five plus five. That was ten. And four more is eleven, twelve . . . thirteen, fourteen." Although he counts the four whites on, he pauses after *twelve* and says *thirteen* and *fourteen* louder, perhaps mentally envisioning the sets of twos. Several children murmur that they did it the same way.

Linda is working toward automaticity here. If children need to, they can count. But she employs several techniques that are likely to stretch children beyond counting. First, she reveals the frame only briefly, then covers it again until they begin to share their strategies. Children who need to count can, and do so, often using their fingers. But the rack supports their coming up with using the five structure and making ten. Linda highlights this as a terrific shortcut and encourages others to use it. She follows up with a good choice of numbers (7 and 7) with which the strategy will be helpful. Other good choices would be 5 + 8 or 6 + 8.

In the following episode, Linda continues her work. This time each child uses his or her own rack.

"So let's get in a circle, and I'll pass the racks out." Linda stands by a large dry-erase board as the children form a circle, with her as a part of it. She passes out the racks and asks them to figure out 7 + 6. On the board she draws an open rack—two lines with no beads—while she gives children time to figure the problem out on their racks. Then she starts the discussion. "Mike, how did you do it? How many reds on top?"

"Five," Mike responds, "and two whites."

Linda draws five red beads on the open rack on the board. "What color shall I use for the whites? White won't show up."

"Blue," several children chorus, and she draws two blue beads next to the five red.

"And it's five reds and one white on the bottom," Mike continues.

Linda completes the drawing and asks, "And so how did you figure out how many it was all together?"

Mike explains that he counted 2, 4, 6 (moving two beads each time), then 7, 8, 9, 10, 11, 12, 13. Linda records his thinking (see Figure 6.4a).

Belinda also offers a counting strategy, although she counts on from seven. Linda records her strategy also (see Figure 6.4b).

"Lorene, what about you?" Linda draws another open rack on which to record Lorene's solution.

"I knew seven plus seven was fourteen, so I just took one away and that made thirteen."

"Wow, Lorene. What a great strategy. Did that make sense to you, Dean?" Linda attempts to pull Dean, who looks puzzled, into the conversation. Dean struggles to paraphrase Lorene's strategy but cannot.

Lorene explains again. "I just knew that seven plus seven was fourteen." Linda draws seven and seven on the open rack. "And then I took one away, that made thirteen." Linda draws an *x* over one bead to represent Lorene's thinking (see Figure 6.4c).

"Oh, I get it," Dean smiles, "that's cool." He tries to explain his earlier puzzlement. "I had mine the other way around. I had six on the top and seven on the bottom."

"Does that matter?" Linda puts the question to everyone.

"No," says Kristi, who is sitting near Dean. "See, if you take one off the top and put it on the bottom, it's still the same amount." She demonstrates by turning $7 + 6$ into $6 + 7$. Dean says he agrees with her reasoning.

In this second episode, we see children grappling with the big idea of the *commutative property of addition* ($6 + 7 = 7 + 6$) and, once again, with the logic of *compensation*. The arithmetic rack supports the use of counting strategies, even counting by twos and counting on, but it also stretches children to give up these counting strategies, grapple with big ideas, and restructure their counting strategies in favor of better shortcuts, like using double plus or minus.

"Well, you guys all have wonderful ways of thinking about this problem," Linda says, moving from the minilesson into the heart of math workshop. "I made books for each of you with lots of problems in them. And I

FIGURE 6.4a
Mike's strategy

FIGURE 6.4b
Belinda's strategy

FIGURE 6.4c
Lorene's strategy

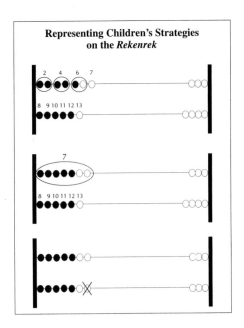

**Representing Children's Strategies
on the *Rekenrek***

drew empty arithmetic racks on each page for you, like I did on the board when I was recording your thinking. Today during math workshop we'll work on our books. Draw a picture of how you solve each problem. You can even write a little about your strategy on each page. And Lorene, you might want to check out whether your strategy of using a double and taking one away will be helpful for any of these problems."

Using the Rekenrek with Contexts and Routines

Thus far, the examples of the *rekenrek* in action have all been devoid of context. We do not want to imply that context is not important or that the arithmetic rack cannot be used with context. On the contrary, it lends itself well to rich contexts and models.

In New York City, as in London and other parts of the world, double-decker buses are frequently used to take tourists on sight-seeing trips. Riders can choose whether to sit on the top, which is open to the air, or on the bottom, which is enclosed. The arithmetic rack is a great manipulative for children to use as a tool to solve situations like these:

> *Seventeen people get on an empty bus. The bus driver sees that nine sat downstairs. How many are up top?*
> *There are seven people up top and six below when the bus stops. Four more people get on. How many are on the bus now?*
> *Let's make our own bus storybooks.*

Bunk beds are another wonderful context easily modeled with the arithmetic rack. Anne Giordano and Carla Middough came up with this context and the children loved it. They told a group of first graders about some kids that had a pajama party. They were all on the bunk beds listening to music. Here again, scenarios of on and off, moving from top to bottom, were designed, providing rich contexts for addition and subtraction. Other situations in the lives of children can also be found and used to provide rich contexts for mathematizing.

The ideas behind the development of the arithmetic rack—supporting and stretching the invented strategies of children by using moveable objects, two sets of five (making ten) on each line—can also be employed with many classroom routines.

Madeline Chang and Diane Jackson both turned their attendance charts into large arithmetic racks. They made pockets that hung on a clothesline and thus could be moved. Five pockets on each line were blue; five were red. Diane had a class of eighteen preschoolers, so she used two lines of ten pockets. Madeline had a class of twenty-eight children, so she used three rows of ten. Each line of ten was broken into two groups of fives. Children were asked to place a paper doll with their name on it in a pocket on any row when they came into class in the morning. During the morning meeting, they discussed how many children were in school. Let's listen in as Madeline and her students discuss that day's attendance. (Figure 6.5 shows the attendance chart). Madeline begins.

"So let's all look at the attendance chart. How many kids are here today? Felicia?"

"Twenty-seven, because there are fifteen here [*pointing to the three groups of five blue pockets*] and then I went sixteen, seventeen, eighteen [. . .] twenty-seven [*counting on to twenty-seven, pointing to each red pocket*]." (See Figure 6.6a.)

"Oh, you didn't start counting from one, you counted on from fifteen," Madeline paraphrases Felicia. Then she asks other children to do the same to check their understanding. "Who knows what Felicia did? Sally?" Sally paraphrases and Madeline continues, "Yes, isn't that neat? Felicia saved herself a lot of counting! Did anyone do it a different way? Sadie?"

Sadie goes to the chart and moves one white pocket over to the left on the top row. In the second row, she moves over two white pockets, and in the third she also moves over two. She explains, "Now I have twenty, because I made another five here." She points to the white pockets that she moved on each line—one, two, and two. "There are seven over there." She points to the white pockets remaining to the right of the ones moved—three, three, and one. "Twenty and seven are twenty-seven," she concludes with certainty. (See Figure 6.6b.)

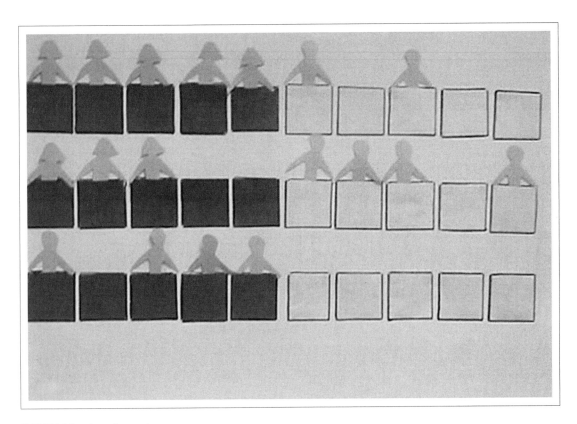

FIGURE 6.5 *Attendance chart*

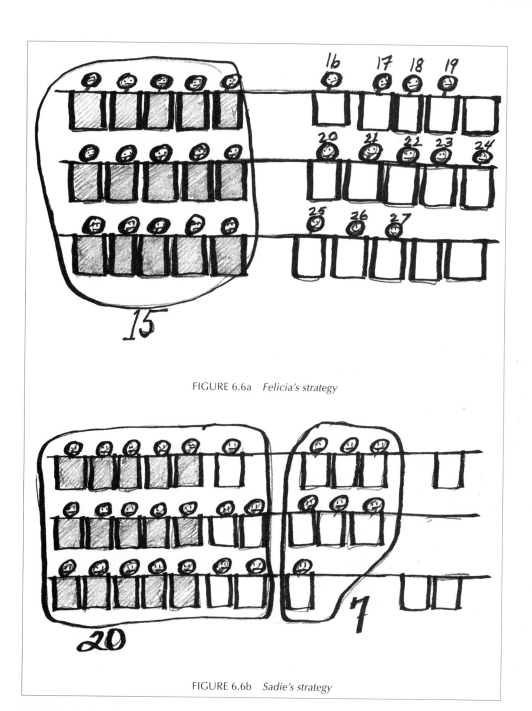

FIGURE 6.6a   *Felicia's strategy*

FIGURE 6.6b   *Sadie's strategy*

FIGURE 6.6   *Attendance strategies*

"No," says Albert. "I disagree. I got twenty-eight."

"Show us, Albert."

Albert shifts one doll from the bottom to the top, making two groups of ten. "See, I made twenty, too. There's eight on the bottom line . . . oh no, I made a mistake. It is twenty-seven." As Albert double-checks his counting on the bottom line, he corrects himself. He does not make use of the five and two, but instead counts every doll on the bottom row one by one.

In this excerpt, we see how the children group and regroup flexibly, making use of fives and tens; yet some still ignore the structure of the material and try to count one by one. Over time, after using the arithmetic rack in many contexts, however, children journey toward the horizon of automatized facts. Strategies do not change overnight. This is hard work. But as these young mathematicians work, they are grappling with big ideas; they are developing efficient strategies, and they are constructing mental maps of number relationships.

SUMMING UP . . .

In *Through the Looking Glass*, the White Queen asks Alice, "Can you do addition? What's one and one and one and one and one and one and one and one and one and one?" Alice responds, "I don't know. I lost count." Like the White Queen, children begin thinking about addition by relying on counting individual units. To go beyond this initial counting strategy they must construct various big ideas and alternative strategies. When adding larger amounts, counting is insufficient. For example, to add all of the White Queen's ones with a strategy other than counting, one must group them into 4 and 4 and 2, or two 5s, etc. Strategies such as these are based on number sense.

Once children understand the big ideas involved in the operations of addition and subtraction, and can model various situations, it is important that they automatize the basic facts. In contrast to memorization, automaticity is accomplished by developing relationships among the facts, leaving far fewer facts to memorize. Repetitive drill and practice and the use of flashcards will not develop an understanding of relationships.

Facts that do need to be memorized are doubles and combinations that make ten, because they are the basis for critical landmark strategies such as double plus or minus, making tens, using compensation, and using other known facts.

Manipulatives like cubes or other counting materials do not necessarily support the development of these strategies; nor do structured materials like Cuisenaire rods. The *rekenrek* is a Dutch calculating frame that was specifically designed to support the development of children's addition and subtraction strategies. It can be used in minilessons or with contexts and routines. As children work with it, they are able to use strategies like double plus or minus, making tens, and compensation—they develop a better sense of the *relationships* among numbers. And it is the automaticity of facts and the development of number relationships that form the basis for efficient calculating and the further development of number theory.

Arithmetique

Monstrat ars numeri que virtus possit habere
Explico pernumeru que sit proportio rerum

7 | ALGORITHMS VERSUS NUMBER SENSE

We are bombarded with numbers, statistics, advertisements, and other such data every day—on the radio, on television, in the newspaper, and on the Internet. We need good mental ability and good number sense to evaluate advertising claims, estimate quantities, calculate reasonable approximations, verify restaurant checks, figure out change and tips, and interpret data and statistics.

We also need to be able to calculate exactly and efficiently. When faced with long columns of numbers to add, we reach for a calculator. But we often need to calculate smaller amounts, two- and three-digit numbers, on the run. Should we have to take out pencil and paper? Is the algorithm the best strategy to use? What do people do who do not use algorithms? What does it mean to calculate with number sense?

Try an experiment. Calculate 3,996 + 4,246. Don't read on until you have an answer.

If you are like most people who are a product of the American school system, you probably got a pencil and paper, rewrote the numbers over in columns, added the units and carried, then added each remaining column, right to left. You used the carrying algorithm—the procedures you were taught in school. If you didn't, congratulations! You probably have "number sense."

What would someone with good number sense do? What would a mathematician do? Both would *look at the numbers first* to decide on a strategy. Because 3,996 is so close to the more "friendly" number 4,000, a more efficient strategy would be to remove 4 from 4,246 and make that 4,242. Combining the 4 with 3,996 effectively turns the problem into 4,000 + 4,242—one that is easy to calculate mentally. But what if the numbers aren't so nice and can't be made "friendly" so easily? Say, perhaps 234 + 136? But why not turn this into 235 + 135, or 240 + 140 − 10. Oh, easy . . . it's 370. All right, let's try another. Perhaps 289 + 79? No, that's easy, too! You can turn it into 290 + 80 − 2, or maybe 300 + 80 − 11 − 1: it's 368. Try to find numbers that can't be made friendly—numbers where the algorithm (the carrying procedure) is faster. You will probably discover that the only time the algorithm is the best strategy is when you are trying to calculate long columns of numbers. And today when we have many large numbers to add, we use a calculator.

THE HISTORY OF ALGORITHMS

Algorithms—the borrowing and carrying procedures—were invented by the great Arab mathematician Muhammad ibn Musa al-Khwarizmi in the early part of the ninth century. They replaced the abacus. Once al-Khwarizmi (the Latin name is Algorismus—hence the term *algorithm*) developed the borrowing and carrying procedures based on place value, computations could be carried out directly with a pen and papyrus. Denis Guedj (1996) describes a bit of the history:

> In the Middle Ages computations were carried out on an abacus, also called a computing table, a calculating device resembling a table with columns or ruled horizontal lines; digits were represented by counters, or apices. From the 12th century on, this type of abacus was progressively replaced by the dust board as a tool of calculations. This development did not come about without a struggle between those who, evoking the ancient Greek mathematician Pythagoras, championed the abacus and those who became masters of algorism, the new Arabic number system. In this competition between the Ancients and Moderns, the former saw themselves as the keepers of the secrets of the art of computation and the defenders of the privileges of the guild of professional calculators. . . . [while] the new system indisputably marked the democratization of computation. (53–54)

The big advance the algorithms brought about was a shift from calculation on a device to a written representation of the calculation. The power of the procedures was that they produced a record of the actions—results could be checked. And calculating was no longer restricted to the guild of professional calculators.

Arithmetical procedures and the computational writing that documented them became the hallmark of knowledge during the Renaissance. Because these skills were required in the marketplace, they became the focus of instruction for youth. A tapestry depicting Lady Arithmetic teaching the algorithms to guild youths hangs in the Cluny Museum in Paris. The algorithms have continued to be the goal of arithmetic instruction in our schools ever since, primarily because until the proliferation of calculators, they were the fastest, most efficient way to compute long columns.

Although the borrowing and carrying procedures are still helpful today for long columns of figures, or when working with numbers that have many digits or that can't be played with easily, they are not the best strategies to use most of the time. Children do have to be able to assess whether the answer on the calculator is reasonable. They also have to have good mental arithmetic strategies. They do need to know how to calculate efficiently. Nevertheless, the hallmark of educated people today is not whether they can perform the algorithms, but how good they are at calculating math mentally. Can they decompose and tinker with numbers? Like the mathematicians, can they turn "unfriendly" problems into "friendly" ones? Can they quickly calculate their share of the restaurant bill mentally, or do they pass the check like a "hot potato" around the table hoping someone else will do it? Can they calculate change quickly when they pay a cashier?

Many schools today are still teaching the algorithms as if proficiency in them is the main goal of elementary mathematics instruction. They are still teaching to the goal of seventeenth-century mathematics education! How do we turn this around? How do we teach for number sense? How do we give our children a chance to be mathematicians?

TEACHING FOR NUMBER SENSE

Old Notions

"You can turn numbers around, when you add," Russell, a second grader, explains to his teacher. "See, 6 + 3 = 9, and 3 + 6 = 9."

"Can you do that with subtraction?" his teacher asks.

Russell looks puzzled.

The teacher writes 7 − 5 and 5 − 7 on the board. Russell begins to beam. "Sure," he says. "7 − 5 = 2, and 5 − 7? That's 2, also!"

The teacher takes out Unifix cubes and says, "Can you show me with these?"

Russell counts out seven, then removes two, and counts the five remaining. "See," he says with assurance.

"What about this one?" The teacher points to 5 − 7.

Once again Russell looks puzzled, but then shrugs, saying, "You just can't do this one with those!"

Let's examine Russell's number sense. To him, it is perfectly possible that there would be no connection between the problem he had solved

$(5 - 7 = 2)$ and a representation with cubes. While on one level, he is correct—it is difficult to show -2 with cubes—on another level, he is sure the answer is two. The sadder issue at hand here is that to him math is something you do with symbols on the board. It does not have to have a connection to reality.

Many years ago, mathematics educators thought teaching for number sense meant helping children like Russell connect their actions to real objects. When it came to teaching addition and subtraction with larger numbers, we used base ten blocks and chip-trading activities to help children understand borrowing and carrying. We taught the traditional algorithms, but we tried to teach what they meant as well. We bundled straws, Popsicle sticks, or other units into tens, and we tried to develop a connection for children between the actions of regrouping the objects and the symbolic notation in the algorithms. We talked about the connection between the concrete, the pictorial, and the symbolic. If we could help Russell, and children like him, see that math could be done with objects first and then be represented with symbols, we thought that we had succeeded in teaching number sense.

The Chinese Approach

Liping Ma (1999) compared the way Chinese teachers think about and teach computation algorithms to the way American teachers usually proceed. Chinese teachers are far more aware of the mathematics in the regrouping than are American teachers; American teachers usually teach the algorithms as a series of procedures. Even when they use manipulatives, they proceed step by step, demonstrating and explaining the regrouping. They focus on helping children line up numbers in columns, and treat these columns one at a time. In contrast, Chinese teachers first develop a deep understanding of expanded notation and equivalence. For example, they focus on how $141 = 100 + 40 + 1 = 100 + 30 + 11$, and on how $19 = 10 + 9$. Then when solving $141 - 19$, learners have a good sense of why it works to borrow and take 9 from 11, and so on.

One could argue that if we taught the algorithms conceptually rather than procedurally, more understanding would result. That is probably true. But in today's world, do we want learners to solve $141 - 19$ like that? Do we want them to use the borrowing algorithm? Why not turn the problem into $142 - 20$? The answer is then apparent without any borrowing at all!

Children's Struggles and Their Inventions

Let's return to our original problem: $3,996 + 4,246$. Now, even if you didn't use the traditional carrying algorithm, go back and use it. But this time, let's look at it step by step. Cover up all the numbers except the units, because the algorithm calls for working with the units first. When you add 6 and 6, notice that you have to put aside, at least momentarily, the concept of the thousands of which they are a part. And because of this you have no idea yet what the answer will be, not even a ballpark estimate! But let's go on. Because 12 is too big for the ones column, write down the 2 and carry the 1 to the tens column. Now uncover the tens column, but keep the last two columns covered. Now add 9 + 4, plus the 1 that was carried. Of course we know that these are really tens, but don't think of it as 90 + 40, add it as 9 + 4 + 1. Notice how, once again, you have to give up thinking about the whole quantities you are adding as you focus on the digits, 9 + 4. Continue in this fashion until you complete the algorithm. Now ask yourself whether you have the right answer. If this is the way you always add, then the only way to know is to go back and do the steps again to check.

Remembering all the steps is difficult for children. But even more difficult is *understanding* the steps and the place value being brought into play. With the algorithm the numbers are not treated as quantities; they are treated as digits. Think of a child who might have made a place value error in calculating the prior problem. When she goes back to check her answer, she's likely to repeat the same error: she's just repeating the procedures, not thinking about the reasonableness of the answer. If she doesn't repeat the error and gets a different answer, she still doesn't know which answer is correct. Everything seems reasonable. So she does it a third time, sometimes with yet a third answer. And often these answers are way off from any reasonable estimate because the error is a place value one. Why do so many children make place value errors? The answer is easily understood when one looks at how nonsensical these "ciphering" steps must seem to a child. Remember that children of this age are also struggling to understand how much 3,996 is. And now we tell them that when they are adding they must start with units—the smallest part of the number!

Most children, and for that matter most humans (unless they have been taught the algorithm), prefer to start with the largest amounts—the thousands. Kamii (1989) found that when children who had not been taught the algorithm were invited to find a way to add these numbers, most split the numbers into the place value components and started with 3,000 + 4,000 = 7,000. Notice how already, in only one step, they have a reasonable estimate of the answer. As a second step, they add 900 + 200 by turning it into 1000 + 100. So far this results in 8,100. Now notice how close they are to a reasonable result. Next we have 90 + 40, which is solved by turning it into 100 + 30, resulting in a total so far of 8,230. The last step is, of course, 6 + 6, with a final answer of 8,242.

Both the formal algorithm and this "splitting" strategy have the same number of steps, so an argument cannot be made that one is faster than the other. The algorithm only seems faster to adults who have practiced it for so

True!

many years that it has become a habit. The algorithm does require less paper (if one assumes that paper is used in both cases as a way to keep track). While this might have been important when paper or papyrus was hard to come by, this is certainly not a consideration today.

A subtraction problem, such as $9,003 - 2,988$, makes this point even clearer. Using the algorithm, I must start with $3 - 8$. Uh, oh. I must be careful . . . it is not $8 - 3$. I must go to the tens column and borrow. Ugh! There is a zero. So I go to the hundreds column and borrow. Ugh! Another zero! Okay, I will borrow from the 9, that makes 8. Now I have 10 hundreds, but I need to make that 9 so now I have 10 tens. Now . . . finally I can borrow from the tens and make that 9 so that I have 13 ones. Now I can subtract 13 $- 8$. Next is $9 - 8$; then $9 - 9$; then $9 - 2$. Finally I'm done, with an answer of 6,015. Am I right? Maybe I should check it again. Compare those procedures with the following, in which 12 is added to both numbers to make them friendlier: $9,003 - 2,988 = 9,015 - 3,000 = 6,015$.

Teaching Computation via Children's Inventions

Because children struggle to understand algorithms and because they can and do invent procedures that demonstrate good number sense, in the 1980s educators began to discuss whether the goal of arithmetic computation should be algorithms at all. Kamii's research leads her to the strong stance that algorithms are actually harmful to children's mathematical development (Kamii and Dominick 1998). First, she examined children's invented procedures for column addition and subtraction and found that children's procedures always went from left to right, from the largest units to the smallest. Since the algorithms go from right to left, children necessarily had to give up their own meaning making in order to perform them. As children were beginning to construct place value, the algorithms actually hindered understanding, and they made children dependent on the spatial arrangement of digits (on paper and pencil) and on other people. Second, Kamii compared the answers that second-, third-, and fourth-grade children gave for problems such as $7 + 52 + 186$, and $504 - 306$. Three groups of children were compared: those that had been taught traditional algorithms only, those that had been taught none (only invented procedures were elicited), and those that had been taught a mixture (in most cases parents taught the algorithm, the teacher did not).

Kamii's data on the first problem with second graders is presented in Figure 7.1. Only 12 percent of the children in the "algorithm" group got the right answer, compared with 26 percent of the "some algorithms" group and 45 percent of the "no algorithms" group. But even more interesting is the range of answers they gave. Answers in the "algorithm" group ranged from 9,308 to 29! In comparison, almost all the answers in the "no algorithm" group were in close proximity to the answer. It appears that most of the errors in the first group were place value errors; in the latter group, they were calculation errors. This is strong evidence that the algorithm actually works against the development of children's understanding of place value and of number sense. As they focus on doing the procedures correctly, they sacrifice their own meaning making; they sacrifice an understanding of the quantity of the numbers they are dealing with.

Writing the problems vertically rather than horizontally made little difference. The subtraction problem (504 − 306) was written vertically. Most second and third graders in the "no algorithms" group said, "Five hundred take away three hundred is two hundred, four take away six is two less than zero, so the answer is one hundred and ninety-eight." Seventy-four percent of the second graders and 80 percent of the third graders in

harmful

Answers to 7 + 52 + 186: Second Graders		
Algorithms *n* = 17	**Some Algorithms** *n* = 19	**No Algorithms** *n* = 20
9308		
1000		
989		
986		
938	989	
906	938	
838	810	
295	356	617
		255
		246
245 (12%)	245 (26%)	245 (45%)
		243
		236
		235
200	213	138
198	213	—
30	199	—
29	133	—
29	125	—
—	114	
—	—	
—	—	
—	—	

FIGURE 7.1 *Kamii's data*

that group got the correct answer. Other wrong answers were close and were calculation errors, not place value errors. In the "algorithms" group, only 42 percent of second graders and 35 percent of third graders got the correct answer, and the range of wrong answers was again enormous! It is also interesting that the group that was taught the algorithms at home did worse than the children who were taught no algorithms at all! Parents often think that if they teach the algorithms, they are helping their children. Kamii's data are evidence that this is not the case. The algorithms that parents teach or, worse, that they hire tutors to teach to their children, actually get in the way of children's learning. As the children try to learn the procedures, they stop thinking about the numbers. They adopt the procedures that their parents show them because they require little thinking. In contrast, children who are not taught algorithms get better and better at decomposing and tinkering with numbers. They become better and better mathematical thinkers. The process takes time; it does not happen overnight. But it does happen.

Calculating with Number Sense

It isn't enough to allow children to invent their own strategies, however. Although children's invented strategies do become more efficient over time, their strategies are remarkably similar—most are based on some form of splitting the number into place value components—that is, 534 is split into $500 + 300 + 4$. Other strategies that mathematicians use frequently, powerful ones like keeping one number whole, are rarely constructed. For example, when adding $368 + 208$, it is more efficient to keep 368 whole and add 200, then 8, than it is to add $200 + 300 + 60 + 16$, yet most children invented the latter strategy. It is also more efficient to turn the problem into $370 + 206$. With subtraction, children rarely invent a strategy we call "constant difference," meaning that the difference between the numbers is kept constant but the numbers are made friendlier—for example, $71 - 36 = 70 - 35 = 35$. Seventy minus 35 is friendly because the double of $35 + 35$ is often known. Another example would be $342 - 37$. It can be turned into $345 - 40$. The difference remains the same, but the problem is "friendlier."

The primary reason children initially use splitting strategies is because problems are most often presented vertically and because math education focuses on place value relationships. In the Mathematics in the City program, we looked seriously at how we could develop a repertoire of computation strategies in children based on number relationships and operations. We began to question whether informal splitting strategies were sufficient to replace the algorithms. While we agreed with Kamii that algorithms hinder the development of number sense, if mathematicians compose and decompose numbers using a host of strategies, how do we ensure that children are developing a *repertoire*? If calculating with number sense means to look at the numbers first to decide on a strategy, rather than applying the same strategy across problems regardless of the numbers, then how do we teach children to do this? How do we encourage children to see patterns and relationships in number and to derive enjoyment from decomposing elegantly? How do we engage them in computing like mathematicians?

To be able to compute with number sense, we have to have a mental model of the relationship between numbers; we have to be able to picture a space—an imaginary number space—with the properties of distance and nearness, surrounding and neighborhood (Lorenz 1997). The repertoire of strategies is not just a list of strategies to choose from when calculating. The strategies are derived from operating flexibly in this number space—from looking at the numbers first, setting up relationships, and then playing with these relationships.

Over the last eight years or so Mathematics in the City has been developing mental math minilessons, as part of math workshop, to help children construct mental models—imaginary number spaces comprising relationships. The starting point of any computation work needs to be children's own constructions. To teach any strategy, including algorithms, directly by focusing on the procedures will only cause children to adopt the procedures and stop thinking. But teachers do have a role in ensuring that efficient strategies are being developed, in ensuring that children are not left with only their initial inventions, such as inefficient splitting. Chapter 8 describes the techniques we have been using and the relationships and strategies—the number space—we try to develop for addition and subtraction.

SUMMING UP . . .

Algorithms were developed in the Middle Ages by the Arab mathematician al-Khwarizmi. The use of algorithms brought about a democratization of computation; people were no longer reliant on the select few who were competent users of the abacus. When algorithms appeared, political tension occurred between those who wanted to hold on to the abacus and those who wanted to learn the new methods. Interestingly, a similar political situation exists today. As schools have begun to reform their teaching, as algorithms have been replaced with mental math strategies and calculating with number sense, arguments have occurred between those who fight to maintain the "old" math and those who favor reform. Many articles have appeared in newspapers that play into fears that children will not be able to compute. These fears are based on uninformed, often mistaken, notions of the reform. Parents are products of the old education, and therefore they define mathematics as the skills they were taught. When they don't see their children learning what they believe to be the goals of mathematics—the algorithms— they assume that nothing is being learned. Many of them have called the new mathematics "fuzzy" or "soft," described it as a "dumbing down."

Algorithms—a structured series of procedures that can be used across problems, regardless of the numbers—do have an important place in mathematics. After students have a deep understanding of number relationships and operations and have developed a repertoire of computation strategies, they may find it interesting to investigate why the traditional computation algorithms work. Exploring strategies that can be used with larger numbers or long columns is an interesting inquiry—one in which the traditional algorithms can be employed. Often algorithms come up in classroom discussions, too, because parents have taught them to their children and children attempt to use them without understanding why they work. Exploring them, figuring out why they work, may deepen children's thinking. There is no need to avoid discussing them.

They should not be the primary goal of computation instruction, however. Using algorithms, the same series of steps with all problems, is antithetical to calculating with number sense. Calculating with number sense means that one must look at the numbers first and then decide on a strategy that is fitting—and efficient. Children who learn to think, rather than to apply the same procedures by rote regardless of the numbers, will be empowered. They will not see mathematics as a dogmatic, dead discipline, but as a living, creative one. They will thrive on inventing their own rules, because these rules will serve afterward as the foundation for solving other problems.

By abandoning the rote teaching of algorithms, we are not asking children to learn less, we are asking them to learn more. We are asking them to mathematize, to think like mathematicians, to look at the numbers before they calculate, to think rather than to perform rote procedures. To paraphrase Plato, we are asking children to act as "free men" in their treatment of arithmetic. Children can and do construct their own strategies, and when they are allowed to make sense of calculations in their own ways, they understand better. In the words of the mathematician Blaise Pascal, "We are usually convinced more easily by reasons we have found ourselves than by those which have occurred to others."

In moving away from algorithms, we are asking teachers to think mathematically, too. We are asking them to develop their own mental math strategies in order to develop them in their students. Once again teachers are on the edge, not only the edge between the structure and development of mathematics, but also the edge between the old and the new—between the expectations of parents and the expectations of the new tests and the new curricula.

The backlash is strong, and walking this edge is difficult. Teachers need our support. Learning to teach in a way that supports mathematizing—in a way that supports calculating with number sense—takes time. Sometimes, as teachers have attempted to reform their practice, children have been left with no algorithms and no repertoire of strategies, only their own informal, inefficient inventions. The reform will fail if we do not approach calculation seriously, if we do not produce children who can calculate efficiently. Parents will define our success in terms of their old notions of mathematics. They saw the goal of arithmetic, of school mathematics, as calculation. They will look for what they know, for what they learned, for what they define as mathematics.

8 | DEVELOPING EFFICIENT COMPUTATION WITH MINILESSONS

I think, therefore I am. . . . Each problem that I solved became a rule which served afterwards to solve other problems.

—*René Descartes,* Discours de la Methode

Mathematics is the only instructional material that can be presented in an entirely undogmatic way.

—*Max Dehn, quoted in* The Mathematical Intelligencer

MINILESSONS WITH MENTAL MATH STRINGS

"I broke the fifteen into a ten and a four and a one." Brittani, a second grader in New York City, is explaining how she solved the problem 15 + 9. "Then I gave the one to the nine, that made ten . . . and I knew that ten plus ten was twenty, and four more made twenty-four."

Jennifer DiBrienza, Brittani's teacher, is beginning math workshop, as she normally does each day, with a short ten- or fifteen-minute minilesson focusing on computation strategies. In contrast to investigations, which characterize the heart of math workshop, the minilessons are more guided and more explicit. They are designed specifically to highlight certain strategies and to develop efficient mental math computation. Each day, Jennifer chooses a string of four or five related problems and asks her students to solve them and share their strategies with one another.

Crucial to Jennifer's choice of problems is the relationship between them. She picks problems that are likely to develop certain strategies or big ideas that she knows are important because they are landmarks on the landscape of learning. We call these groups of problems *strings* because they are a structured series of problems that are related in such a way as to develop and highlight number relationships and operations.

Choosing the Strategies, Choosing the Numbers

The string that Jennifer is using is shown in Figure 8.1. Jennifer has chosen these numbers to encourage children to make use of ten when they add. Ten can be helpful in several ways:

1. By taking leaps of ten all at once and correcting—for example, 15 + 9 = 15 + 10 − 1.
2. By moving to the next nearest ten—for example, 15 + 9 = 15 + 5 [to get 20, the next nearest ten] + 4.
3. By using compensation to make a problem with ten in it—for example, 15 + 9 = 14 + 10.

Jennifer begins with 15 + 10 and then moves to 15 + 9, because the number 9 is so close to 10. She anticipates that some children will notice that and will make a leap of ten and subtract one, effectively bringing the strategy up for discussion. The third problem is related to the second in that 19 is 10 more than 9. Here Jennifer anticipates that whatever strategy her students have found effective in the second problem will be extended in the third. If children simply count, and do not use the ten, patterns will still appear in the answers that are likely to engender discussion. Her fourth problem (28 + 19) she hopes will challenge them further. Will children turn the problem into 28 + 20 − 1 or into 30 + 17? The next problem (28 + 32) is similar; will they do 28 + 30 + 2 or make the problem 30 + 30? In the last problem (39 + 21), she hopes that even children who were not initially making use of the tens will do so here, after the discussion. Thirty-nine is so close to 40, and 21 is so close to 20. She anticipates that many children now will see how easy it is to turn the problem into 40 + 20.

Although Jennifer has thought about the problems beforehand and has a string of related problems ready, she does not put all the problems on the board at once. Instead she writes one at a time, and children discuss their strategies before the subsequent problem is presented. This way, the children can consider the strategies from the prior problem as well as the numbers, and they are prompted to think about the relationships of the problems in the string as they go along. Sometimes, depending on the strategies she hears, Jennifer adjusts the problems in her planned string on the spot to en-

FIGURE 8.1
Jennifer's string

sure that the strategies she is attempting to develop are discussed and tried out. For example, if none of the children make ten when they solve 15 + 9, Jennifer might continue to use ten explicitly—27 + 10, 32 + 10—and then return to the 9 with a problem like 32 + 9.

Brittani is beginning to make tens, but to do so she splits the 15 up into three numbers (10 + 4 + 1)—a slower, more cumbersome strategy. For just that reason, Jennifer begins the discussion with this strategy and uses it as a scaffold for more efficient strategies.

Tools, Representations, and Models

After Brittani shares her strategy, Jennifer paraphrases, drawing three short lines from the number 15 to represent the split. "So you broke up the fifteen into ten, four, and one." She writes these numbers under the 15 (see Figure 8.2). "Then you made another ten with the one and the nine." She draws lines connecting these numbers. "And then you added the tens to make twenty, and the four left made twenty-four?"

By representing children's strategies, Jennifer provides a written record of the action. This allows other children to "see" the strategy; it becomes a picture that can be discussed. It is often too difficult for children to understand purely verbal explanations, particularly when the strategy being described is different from the one they used. Having a picture of the action allows more children to understand and to take part in the discussion.

"Any questions for Brittani? Did anybody do it a different way? Luke?"

"I used the hundreds chart," Luke points to the large pocket chart containing the numbers 1 through 100 that Jennifer has hanging adjacent to the chalkboard, "and I took one away."

Although Jennifer's goal is to *develop* mental math strategies, that does not mean that during the minilesson children must *use* mental strategies. Although Brittani has solved the computation mentally, Luke has not.

"Show us, Luke," Jennifer says.

"I started with fifteen, and I jumped down a row to twenty-five. Then I took one away." Luke points to the numbers on the chart as he explains.

Although Jennifer knows why he took one away, she is aware that for

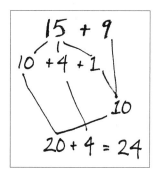

FIGURE 8.2
Representation of
Brittani's strategy

many of her beginning second graders this is a difficult leap in thinking. So she asks Luke to elaborate. "Tell us why you took one away."

Although Luke is clear why he took one away, he struggles to communicate his reasoning to his classmates. "Because I knew fifteen plus ten was twenty-five, but I needed to take one away." Other children begin to question him.

"But why, Luke?" Katia asks, puzzled. "How did you know to take one away?"

This time he is clearer as he responds. "Because I only needed nine, not ten." Several children, including Katia and Brittani, now nod with understanding and agreement.

Although Luke has not solved the problem mentally—he has used the hundreds chart as a tool—his strategy is very efficient. He has kept the fifteen whole and made use of the fact that nine is so close to ten. He takes a leap of ten all at once and subtracts one at the end. Because the hundreds chart is structured in tens, children often notice the patterns and begin to move vertically on it rather than horizontally. When they move vertically they are taking leaps of ten; when they move horizontally they are counting by ones. Although they notice and use the patterns on the hundreds chart, they are not necessarily thinking of leaps of ten mentally, however. This is an important landmark strategy—one that Jennifer wants to highlight in this minilesson.

To do so, she models Luke's strategy on the open number line (see Figure 8.3a). She wants to stretch Luke to think in leaps of ten, mentally, on a number line without needing the hundreds chart as a manipulative. By connecting the hundreds chart to the open number line, she attempts to help all the children move from a tool—a model *of* their thinking—to a more formal mathematical model *for* thinking—a number line.

"So you took a leap of ten," she paraphrases as she draws the leap on the number line and writes *10* above it and *25* under it. "And then you went

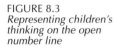

FIGURE 8.3
Representing children's thinking on the open number line

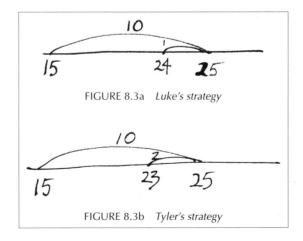

FIGURE 8.3a   *Luke's strategy*

FIGURE 8.3b   *Tyler's strategy*

back one because you only needed to have done nine." Jennifer writes *1* and makes a small leap backward, completing the representation by writing *24*. "Wow, that's a neat strategy, isn't it?" she finishes, inviting the class to reflect on Luke's strategy.

Although Jennifer's next problem in the string she has prepared is 15 + 19, she decides to try 15 + 8 instead. She wants to see whether children will make use of Luke's strategy. "Let's try another problem." Underneath the last problem, which now reads *15 + 9 = 24*, she writes *15 + 8*. "Show me with your thumbs when you have an answer." After giving an appropriate amount of "think time," which she gauges by looking at the number of thumbs up, she starts a discussion. "Tyler?"

"Twenty-three. 'Cause like Luke said . . . he jumped down ten and went back one. That was twenty-four. So I jumped back two."

Jennifer draws an open number line again, this time to represent Tyler's thinking (see Figure 8.3b). "Neat, you used Luke's idea." Luke smiles broadly. "How many of you did it that way?" Several hands go up. "Did anybody do it a different way? Karen?"

Although it seems a simple step to go from 15 + 9 = 24 to 15 + 8 = 24 − 1, and many children do see this relationship, Karen does not. She sees it as a separate problem, and she needs to make sense of it for herself.

"Can I use the arithmetic rack?" Karen points to the fifty Unifix cubes (in groups of five in alternating colors) on each of two strings, one above the other, which Jennifer has made and strung across the top of the chalkboard (similar to the *rekenrek* discussed in Chapter 6).

"Sure," Jennifer says. "What do you want me to put over on the top?"

"Fifteen," Karen responds tentatively.

"Okay, so here's ten." On purpose, Jennifer first slides over two groups of five in order to reinforce children's understanding, and use, of ten. "So how many more do I need?" Will Karen know immediately that five more will be needed, or will she need to count?

"Five more," Karen responds.

"Okay." Jennifer moves them over. "And what do you want on the bottom?"

"Eight."

"Okay, here's ten." Jennifer moves over two groups of five, again attempting to support the development of strategies based on tens. "How can I make this into eight?"

"Take two off," Karen answers and Jennifer moves two back to the right (see Figure 8.4a).

"How many more would finish the next ten up here?" Jennifer points to the top line as she attempts to stretch Karen's thinking toward compensation as well.

"Five more."

"Okay," Jennifer agrees. "So can I just exchange this group of five on the bottom for a group of five on the top? Is it okay to do an even trade?"

Karen agrees, and Jennifer moves five on the bottom line to the right, and then shifts five on the top over to the left, making twenty on the top and three on the bottom (see Figure 8.4b). "So we know it's twenty-three?"

Karen nods, and Jennifer then draws an open number line to represent what they did together on the arithmetic rack, once again moving from a manipulative to a representation of the strategy to a model. "Here's a picture of what we did. We took five from the eight and added it to fifteen. That gave us twenty. Then we had three more to go. That made twenty-three." (See Figure 8.4c.) She gives the children a chance to reflect on the model, then she writes *15 + 19* and goes on with her string.

In her minilesson, Jennifer makes use of several tools, representations, and models. She uses short lines to represent splitting. She uses the open number line to represent the other strategies. Children go back and forth from the hundreds chart to the arithmetic rack to the open number line. While the hundreds chart is likely to encourage the use of leaps of ten, because children can go up and down rows, the arithmetic rack is more likely to support use of the structure of five. But because the hundreds chart and the arithmetic rack allow children to count by ones, they are less likely to encourage children to take leaps to the next complete ten. In contrast, the open number line encourages children to think about landmarks on a line,

FIGURE 8.4a *First step on the* rekenrek *with Karen*

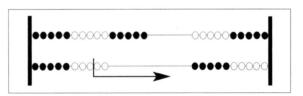

FIGURE 8.4b *Second step on the* rekenrek *with Karen*

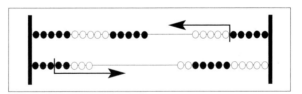

FIGURE 8.4c *Representing the strategy on the open number line*

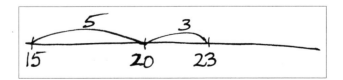

to take the leaps mentally. The hundreds chart does not represent number linearly, as on a number line, but more like prose when one is reading. After ten comes eleven, but one must shift to the left of the next line to find it. This can be a problem for children as they are developing a "number space"—a model to think with.

Although students may initially compute problems in a string in various ways, as they share their strategies they notice and discuss patterns in the string and in the answers. They become intrigued by the fact that answers are the same, or that they are different by one or by ten, and they want to investigate why these patterns are happening. They are impressed by, and interested in, their classmates' strategies and they often adopt them when they seem appropriate and more efficient.

DEVELOPING ADDITION AND SUBTRACTION STRATEGIES

Designing strings and other minilessons to develop a "number space" requires that teachers have a deep sense of number relationships and operations and that they know how to play with numbers so as to facilitate the development of strategies for addition and subtraction. Below we discuss some important strategies, point out the landmarks associated with them, and suggest mental math strings that may facilitate their development.

Series of quick images using manipulatives are powerful strings for the youngest children: they encourage children to give up inefficient counting strategies and search for patterns in the visual array that can be subitized and easily combined. In Chapter 6, we saw Linda Jones uncover a *rekenrek* briefly and then ask children to explain what they saw and how they figured it out. Plastic counters can also be glimpsed briefly with an overhead projector (see Figure 8.5), or large index cards can be used, with stickers on them subitized into groups. The cards can be shown quickly, long enough for students to see the groups but not long enough for them to be able to count each sticker by ones (see Figures 8.6). Whatever is used (the arithmetic rack, the overhead with plastic counters, or index cards), the number choices in and the relationships between the problems are critical.

Doubles and Near Doubles with Addition

A mental math string meant to develop the idea of doubles and near doubles needs to have that relationship built into it. For example, start with a double fact that children are likely to know by heart—5 + 5, for example. Then pick a closely related "almost" double—5 + 6 or 5 + 4 are good choices. Next try another double—7 + 7, for example—and follow with some more near doubles—6 + 7 or 8 + 7. Now throw in a problem that can be made into a double if compensation is used—6 + 8 can become 7 + 7, for example. (This is what we saw Linda Jones doing in Chapter 6.) When working with larger numbers, the idea remains the same. Figure 8.7a shows a string for double plus or minus. The string begins with a double children might know, 25 + 25. The next three problems are related: 25 + 26, 25 + 24, 25 + 28. A second string, shown in Figure 8.7b, begins with 30 + 30. It is followed by a problem that with compensation becomes the double (29 + 31) and two near double problems (28 + 30, 29 + 29).

Splitting

Splitting is a strategy that children develop, almost on their own, as soon as they begin to understand place value. They split the numbers up into friendlier pieces, usually into hundreds, tens, and ones. For example, the problem 28 + 44 might be solved by adding 20 + 40, then 8 + 4, and then combining the whole thing to make 60 + 10 + 2. To add 376 + 243, children

FIGURE 8.5
Quick images on the overhead with chips

FIGURE 8.6
Index card Quick Images

using a splitting strategy will add 300 + 200 + 70 + 40 + 6 + 3. This strategy can best be represented with lines, as in 8.7. and 8.8. Splitting is an important landmark in relation to place value, but it is not a very efficient strategy for mental computation (although it is of course much more efficient than counting).

Making Jumps of Ten

In the jumps-of-ten strategy, one number is kept whole and jumps of ten are added to it—for example, 28 + 44 = 44 + 10 + 10 + 8 (the 8 is usually broken into 6 and 2, to make use of the landmark number 70). This thinking is more easily represented on an open number line (see Figure 8.9). It is the strategy that Luke used and that Jennifer was working on with her string. Children often begin by adding only one ten at a time, although later all the tens are added at once: 44 + 20 + 8. With larger amounts, hundreds (or thousands) are added first. For example, 3,486 + 1,214 = 3,486 + 1,000

FIGURE 8.7a
*Addition strings with
doubles and near
doubles*

25 + 25	30 + 30
25 + 26	29 + 31
25 + 24	28 + 30
25 + 28	29 + 29

FIGURE 8.8
*Representation of
a splitting strategy*

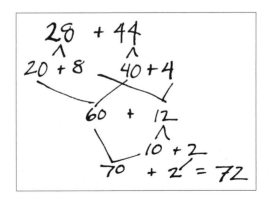

+ 200 + 10 + 4 (see the open number line in Figure 8.10). This is a powerful mental computation strategy and an important landmark.

Figure 8.11 is an example of a mental math string that can be used to encourage the development of this strategy. The first four problems introduce the idea of adding tens or hundreds. The last two problems build on the others. By the end of the string, what would originally have been a difficult problem to do mentally has become an easy one.

Moving to the Next "Friendly" Number

This strategy is closely aligned with the jumps-of-ten strategy but is the reverse, in that the units are added first to reach a friendly number. With a problem like 98 + 37, we want children to notice how close the 98 is to 100 and make use of that friendly number: turning the problem into 100 + 35 makes it very easy to solve. Splitting here is much more cumbersome. First you have to compute 90 + 30, then 8 + 7, then add the totals. Taking leaps of ten, even when done efficiently (98 + 30 + 2 + 5), is also cumbersome.

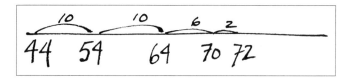

FIGURE 8.9
Making jumps of ten

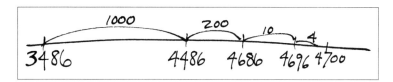

FIGURE 8.10
*3,486 + 1,214 on
an open number line*

63 + 10	143 + 107
43 + 10	138 + 20
123 + 10	138 + 23
143 + 100	138 + 123

FIGURE 8.11
*A string to develop the
jumps-of-ten strategy*

The minute one number is turned into a friendly number, many problems become easy: $27 + 49 = 26 + 50$; $36 + 118 = 34 + 120$; $227 + 164 = 230 + 161$. Carrying is unnecessary, splitting is unnecessary, and leaps of ten are unnecessary. Once the compensation is made, the problem can usually be solved mentally.

Once again, a mental math string intended to develop this strategy needs to begin with a simple problem that will likely elicit it—for example, $38 + 6$. Although some children may count on by ones, many will add 2 in one leap and then add 4. This happens because 38 is close to 40 and 6 is a single-digit number that can be broken up easily. Follow with a larger but related second number, like $38 + 26$ (26 is related to 6 because the units digit is the same). Many children will likely see the relationship and add 20 more. On the open number line this becomes $38 + 2 + 4 + 20$ (see Figure 8.12). Follow with the problem $40 + 24$ to make the strategy even more apparent. Although children will likely solve this problem easily—adding 20 to 40 and then adding 4—the compensation involved becomes more apparent because the answer is the same ($38 + 26 = 40 + 24$). Then try another related series: $47 + 24$, $50 + 21$ or $47 + 4$, $47 + 34$, $50 + 31$. Move on to the hundreds: $100 + 27$ (easy!) followed by $98 + 29$, and $96 + 29$, and $95 + 30$, or $300 + 35$, $298 + 37$, and so on.

FIGURE 8.12
*Moving to a friendly
number*

Swapping

This addition strategy is only helpful in a few situations, but Katia, who initially made a mistake when she was writing down a problem, invented it. She reversed the digits in the units place, writing $32 + 99$ in her math journal instead of $39 + 92$. When the class was discussing strategies and answers, she realized she had written the numbers incorrectly but had gotten the same answer! In fact, her problem was easier because of the 99. (Look at how reversals can help you solve $293 + 919$. Put all the nines in the same number by switching digits and you get $999 + 213$; move to the nearest friendly number and compensate—$1000 + 212 = 1212$—and you're done! No carrying or messy splitting!)

This phenomenon was very intriguing to the children, and the class tried a few more only to find that the answers were once again the same. An even nicer benefit was the big idea that developed as children explored where and why the strategy worked and when using it was beneficial. For example, they discovered that digits could only be swapped in similar place value columns, never across columns—this discovery led to a deeper, richer understanding of place value and the ability to commute the addition within the columns.

Let's visit Jennifer's class again as she uses a mental math string to highlight swapping. (This is the classroom in which Katia invented the strategy. Jennifer is revisiting the idea.) The children have just discussed 25 + 18. Although they have used several strategies, they have all agreed on the answer and Jennifer has written *25 + 18 = 43*. Underneath that she has written *28 + 15* and given the class time to solve it.

Jennifer begins the discussion. "How did you do it, Pedro?"

"I split the twenty-eight into twenty plus eight, and I split the fifteen into ten plus five. Then I split the five into two plus three."

Jennifer paraphrases as she tries to represent his splitting strategy with lines (see Figure 8.13a). "Okay, correct me if I'm wrong. Now you have twenty plus eight plus ten plus two plus three."

"Yep. And then I gave the two to the twenty-eight to make thirty—"

Jennifer interrupts him when she realizes that he really didn't split the 28. "Oh, so you really didn't split the twenty-eight, you kept it whole and added two more to it to make thirty." Pedro agrees, so she draws an open number line (see Figure 8.13b) to represent his thinking. "That's great. It's faster when you keep one number whole, isn't it? Then what did you do?"

"I added ten to get to forty, and then three more to get to forty-three." He is confident of his thinking, but several hands are up.

Jennifer smiles. "Did anybody have a fast way to do it—so fast that they couldn't believe it? Joan?"

"I knew that twenty-five plus eighteen was forty-three, from before." Joan points to the earlier problem on the board. "So twenty-eight plus fifteen is also forty-three!"

Jennifer laughs, "Wow . . . what's that strategy called?"

"Swapping!" Several children call out and look at Katia.

"Yes, it's Katia's swapping strategy." Jennifer acknowledges Katia, who is beaming. "You just swapped the eight and the five, so you knew the answers were the same! You just flipped the ones. So twenty-eight plus fifteen is also forty-three." Jennifer completes the equation.

"Oh, my gosh." Pedro slaps his hand against his head and laughs in

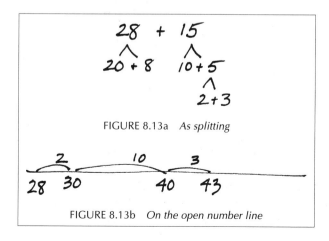

FIGURE 8.13a   *As splitting*

FIGURE 8.13b   *On the open number line*

FIGURE 8.13
Representing Pedro's strategy

recognition. "I just noticed. It's like . . . swapping. I should have known that right away!"

An example of a mental math string to trigger an investigation with children who have not yet constructed the swapping strategy is shown in Figure 8.14. The phenomenon of identical answers, no matter what strategies children use to arrive at them, will usually provoke enough interest that they will want to find out why.

Adding on vs. Removing

Because subtraction is so inherently connected to addition, the strategies are similar. Although an understanding of the relationship between addition and subtraction needs to be developed with contexts first (see Chapter 5), mental math strings can be used afterward to develop mental math computation strategies. For example, with a problem like $62 - 4$, it makes more sense to remove 4, to work backwards from 62. But with the problem $62 - 54$ it makes more sense to add on from 54. When numbers are close together it is easier to add on; when they are far apart, to work backward. If strings are structured with that idea in mind (see Figure 8.15), a rich conversation usually ensues on how both strategies (adding on and removing) are important and can be used to solve subtraction problems, but how, depending on the numbers, one or the other might be a better choice. Some children will work backward with the first two problems in Figure 8.15, then switch their strategy to adding on for the third. This is an opportunity to point out what they've done and ask them to discuss why. It is impor-

FIGURE 8.14
A string to produce an investigation around swapping

$$34 + 19$$

$$39 + 14$$

$$71 + 26$$

$$76 + 21$$

$$449 + 192$$

$$142 + 499$$

$$442 + 199$$

FIGURE 8.15
A string for adding on vs. removing

$$33 - 4$$

$$33 - 7$$

$$42 - 37$$

$$33 - 28$$

tant for children to understand that subtraction problems can be solved with addition strategies. Often teachers make the mistake of telling children that subtraction means "take away." That is only one model of subtraction. Working backward is usually harder for most humans, adults and children, and there is no reason to insist that subtraction problems be treated as removal.

Because subtraction problems are solved with both adding on and removing strategies, they can be represented on the open number line both ways. What we draw should represent what the child has done. For example 343 − 192 might be solved by adding 8 onto 192 to make 200, then adding another 143 to get to 343, for an answer of 151. On the open number line, that looks like addition, as one leaps from 192 to 200 to 343.

On the other hand, working backward can also solve the problem. One could start at 343 and remove 143, then remove 8 more to land on 192. In this case, to represent the child's thinking on the open number line, you must start on the right at 343 and draw a leap to the left. (See Figure 8.16.)

Let's enter Carol Mosesson's third-grade class in New York City, as she presents a minilesson in which she represents children's strategies on open number lines and discusses whether the strategies move backward or forward.

On chart paper Carol writes *175 − 19*. The children are nestled around her on the meeting area rug, math journals in hand. She gives them a few moments to figure the problem out and to record their thinking in their journals, then she asks for answers. Everyone agrees that the answer is 156. Carol begins a discussion by asking Nikisha to explain her strategy.

"I know that 175 take away ten is 165," Nikisha explains. "Take away another ten, that's 155, then plus one, that is 156." She has moved backward in jumps of ten. Carol represents Nikisha's thinking on an open number line (see Figure 8.17a) and asks, "Why did you plus one?"

"I went an extra ten," Nikisha explains, "because ten was the next friendly number, so I had to add the one."

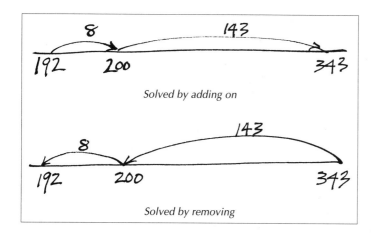

FIGURE 8.16
*Representing strategies
for 343 − 192*

Carol tries to bring out more discussion on this. "Chrystal, do you want to add to that?"

"Yeah, she had an extra one so she had to add it back on."

"That was a fast way to do that, wasn't it? And I hear some people saying Nikisha could have done it an even faster way. Xavier?"

Xavier, who also worked backward, explains, "She could have taken away twenty all at once and then added one on."

Carol uses another open number line to represent Xavier's strategy (see Figure 8.17b). "You're pretty comfortable making jumps of twenty, aren't you? And that is faster. Let's try another problem." Carol writes *175 − 139* and reminds the children, "Thumbs up when you're ready." This time the answers do not agree. Carol writes down all the answers—314, 46, 36, and 44. (By writing all the answers down without acknowledging which is correct, Carol invites the children to keep thinking. They have a chance to evaluate the other answers and the strategies used. They also reflect on their own work again, to check whether they are correct.)

Then she asks Daryll, who has added and gotten 314, to explain his answer. He immediately realizes his error. "It's 314. Oh no, it can't be. I made a mistake. I added."

Carol smiles—it's a common mistake—and moves on. "Other answers are forty-six, thirty-six, and forty-four. Jamal, you got forty-six. Share your thinking."

"I started with 175. I took away 100. Then I had seventy-five and I took away forty to get forty-five." Even though he has made an error, Carol draws exactly what he says on an open number line (see Figure 8.18a). Jamal continues, "Then I plussed one to get forty-six."

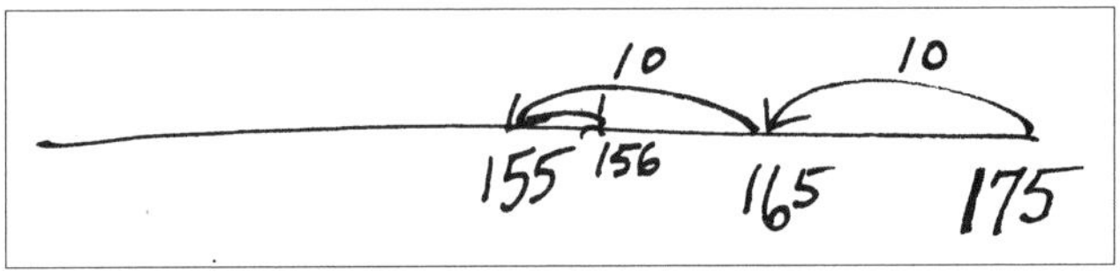

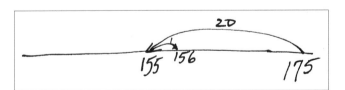

FIGURE 8.17a
Nikisha's strategy for 175 − 19

FIGURE 8.17b
Xavier's strategy for 175 − 19

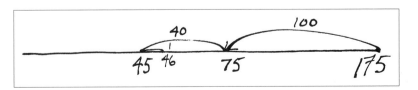

FIGURE 8.18a
Jamal's strategy for 175 − 139

Carol wants to see if other children will pick up the error. "Who can re-peat what Jamal said? Let's look at what he did. Jackie?"

Jackie repeats the series of calculations without noticing the error, and Natalie adds, "Yes. He had to add one because he needed to do 139, and 140 was one too many."

Now Carol draws attention to the error. "Does everyone agree that he did 139? Nikisha?"

"I disagree, because take away 140, take away. . . ." Nikisha struggles at first, then becomes clearer: "no—seventy-five minus forty is thirty-five, not forty-five."

"Oh, yeah . . ." Jamal realizes his error.

Carol asks him, "Are you sure? So what is the final number?"

"Thirty-six," Jamal responds confidently.

Carol not only writes all the answers first, she also processes the thinking behind them. This enables her to see what each child has done and to encourage the children to look at the mistakes in their own and others' thinking. The children determine whether an answer is correct or not, not Carol. This does not mean that Carol abdicates her role in facilitating learning: she prompts the children to analyze each strategy for correctness. Too often teachers forget the role of mistakes in learning and focus only on correct solutions.

Carol moves on, focusing on the next wrong answer. "All right, so let's look at forty-four. Xavier, that was your answer. What did you do?"

He has used an adding-on strategy: "I started at 139. I plussed forty, and then I was at 179. Then I took away four to 175."

Carol draws his thinking on an open number line (see Figure 8.18b) and asks, "So what's your answer?"

He gives his initial answer, but then corrects himself: "Forty-four, no . . . thirty-six."

Carol asks him to explain. "Why thirty-six?"

"Because I plussed forty so I had to take away four. I added the four. I should have subtracted it."

Xavier's explanation gets at the heart of the connection between addition and subtraction, the forward and backward movement on the number line. It is difficult for children to keep track of the compensation when they are subtracting. If they subtract too much, they have to add that amount back in at the end. If they add too much on, they have to subtract that amount at the end. The open number line helps Xavier see his error. Originally it is only a model of his thinking, but over time it will become a model to think with—

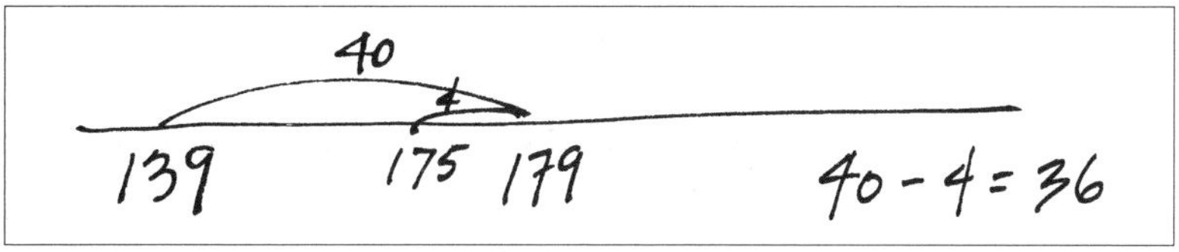

FIGURE 8.18b
Xavier's strategy for
175 − 139

children will be able to envision mentally the backward and forward motion on the line.

Now that the error is corrected and the children agree that the answer is thirty-six, Carol focuses the discussion on her original goal—the relationship between a moving-backward strategy and a moving-forward strategy: "What do you all think of Xavier's way?"

"Real quick," several children respond.

"Yeah."

"Why did he take away before [*referring to the first problem, 175 − 19*] but now [*with 175 − 139*] he is adding on?"

The children ponder this question. Finally Michael responds, "'Cause he was trying to see how much it was from 139 to 175 and that's quicker. He would get the answer faster than taking away 139 from 175."

"What is it about the numbers that made it easier?" Carol asks, encouraging the children to analyze the numbers, to look at them before they decide on a strategy.

Michael continues, "The numbers before were not close together. It was easier to take away. Where they are close, it is easier to add on."

"I agree," Shakina says. "I added on, too. I started at 139 and added on thirty, then six more."

"Nice," comments Carol as she draws the open number line to represent Shakina's thinking (see Figure 8.18c).

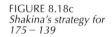

FIGURE 8.18c
Shakina's strategy for 175 − 139

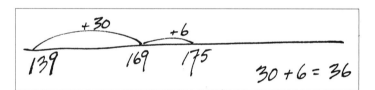

Doubles and Near Doubles with Subtraction

How easily 52 − 25 can be solved when one uses the known double of 25 + 25! Since two is left, the answer is 27. No borrowing is necessary. If doubles have been developed well in addition, children use them easily with subtraction. Figure 8.19 shows a string developed with this relationship in mind. The first problem is a double, the second is a near double, the third is a double, the fourth a near double, and so on.

Making Jumps of Ten Backward

Being able to move backward and forward in jumps of ten or a hundred using a number line is a critical landmark. This knowledge can be extended into a powerful mental math strategy. For example 137 − 84 can be solved by subtracting 30, then 50, then 4, or by adding 20, then 30, then 3.

Figure 8.20 shows a subtraction string meant to support the development of this idea. Notice that the 10 and the 30 are used before the 34 or the 39. This supports and guides the learning. The string is scaffolded to highlight the strategy. Children often begin by taking only one step of ten at a time, and they need to be encouraged to take thirty or forty away at once.

Let's visit Carol Mosesson's class again and watch her develop this strategy in another minilesson. Carol has written $150 - 39$ on a chart. The children are sitting on a rug clustered around her, working in their math journals to solve the problem. "Answers? Jamal?"

"One hundred and eleven."

"Any other answers?"

"One hundred and twenty."

"Any others? Natalie?"

"One hundred and twenty-nine."

"Any other answers?" There is no response. "Then these are all the answers. Okay. Let's look at them. Are any of them unreasonable? Darique?"

"It can't be 120 because 150 minus thirty is 120," Darique responds.

Michael, who has also taken thirty away and then nine more, agrees and adds, "And you have to take another nine away."

$$50 - 25$$

$$52 - 25$$

$$70 - 35$$

$$72 - 35$$

$$40 - 20$$

$$40 - 21$$

$$40 - 19$$

FIGURE 8.19
A subtraction string around doubles and near doubles

$$62 - 10$$

$$62 - 30$$

$$62 - 34$$

$$178 - 10$$

$$178 - 30$$

$$178 - 39$$

FIGURE 8.20
A subtraction string around jumps of tens

Crystal, who had gotten 120, agrees, explaining that she had just forgotten to take away the nine more.

Carol draws the open number line in 8.21a to model Crystal's strategy and then turns to Daryll, whom she knows has done it differently. "Is that how you did it, Daryll?"

"No."

"How did you do it?"

Daryll has done three steps. He explains why. "I know that 150 take away twenty is 130. Then I took away ten more, and then nine."

"Does this represent your thinking?" Carol asks as she draws the open number line in Figure 8.21b.

"Yeah."

"What is the difference between these strategies? Or are they similar? Crystal?"

"They're different," Crystal decides. "Daryll made a jump of twenty. Michael and I made a jump of thirty."

"Calvin, what about you?" Carol attempts to broaden participation.

"I started at 150. I took away ten. That was 140. Then another ten, that was 130. And another ten, that was 120. Then nine, that was 111." Carol draws all these steps on an open number line (see Figure 8.21c).

All three strategies can be characterized as taking leaps of ten. Initially children usually begin with single tens, like Calvin does. As they become more able to move forward and backward in leaps of ten, their strategies become more efficient, like Michael's and Crystal's. Carol wants children to

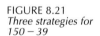

FIGURE 8.21
Three strategies for 150 − 39

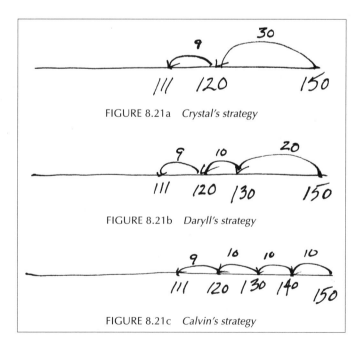

FIGURE 8.21a   *Crystal's strategy*

FIGURE 8.21b   *Daryll's strategy*

FIGURE 8.21c   *Calvin's strategy*

think about the connection between these strategies, and to challenge them to consider efficiency. She continues to focus the discussion on this issue.

"How did Michael see thirty-nine? Aysha?"

"Thirty plus nine."

"And Daryll, how did he see it? Natalie? Jamal?" Carol continues to bring others into the discussion.

"Twenty plus nine."

"Twenty plus nine? Is that thirty-nine?" Carol wonders.

Jamal adds another ten, and Carol writes *10 + 20 + 9*.

"And Calvin," Carol continues, "how did he see thirty-nine?"

"Ten plus ten plus ten plus nine," offers Tarisha.

"So there are all these ways to make thirty-nine," Carol summarizes. "What [strategy] would be the quickest?" After letting the children ponder this question, she calls on Terrance. "What do you think, Terrance?"

"Michael's way."

"Michael's way," Carol repeats. "Why?"

"Because he made just one big jump of thirty."

By encouraging her students to compare strategies and discuss their efficiency, Carol is engaging them in a process that mathematicians follow—the search for efficiency and elegance. Carol values all the thinking, and the culture of the community that she has developed allows children to take risks, to solve problems in their own way. Many of the children may need to take small jumps of ten, and they are allowed to do so. As they discuss and compare the strategies, they become more able to take bigger jumps at once. Rather than feeling that their strategies are inadequate, they feel honored that their classmates are reflecting on them, and they engage in this process themselves, deriving pleasure in the search for efficiency.

Moving to the Next Friendly Ten

A closely related strategy to jumps of ten is moving to the next friendly ten first and then taking leaps of ten backward—for example, solving 143 − 24 by moving three back to 140, then 20 back to 120, then one back to 119. Figure 8.22 shows a mental math string that might bring this strategy to the surface.

$$143 - 3$$
$$143 - 23$$
$$143 - 24$$
$$164 - 25$$
$$182 - 43$$

FIGURE 8.22
A string developed around moving to the next friendly ten

Constant Difference

When we add two numbers, compensation is a common strategy. For example, when adding $49 + 51$ we can add one to the 49 and take away one from 51 to turn the problem into $50 + 50$. This strategy doesn't work with subtraction. With $39 - 21$, if we add one to 39 and take one from 21 to turn the problem into $40 - 20$, we get the wrong answer. When we think of subtraction as the "difference between two numbers" rather than as "take away," it is easy to see why this doesn't work. By turning the problem into $40 - 20$, we expanded the difference between the two numbers by two. To keep the difference constant we have to add (or remove) the *same amount* to both numbers. This is a powerful strategy for subtraction because messy, unfriendly problems can easily be made friendly—for example, $1226 - 189$ can be turned into $1237 - 200$ by adding 11 to each number, $302 - 44$ can be turned into $308 - 50$. Children who have been taught the algorithm make lots of mistakes with these messy problems because so much borrowing or regrouping is needed. Children who understand constant difference and use it rarely make an error.

To understand this strategy, children have to grapple with the big idea of subtraction as difference—as the distance between two points on a number line. Let's return to Carol's class once more and listen as her children discuss this strategy. On the chart is written $175 - 139 = 36$. The children have just finished solving this problem, and Carol has written a new, but related, problem underneath, $174 - 138$. Will the children see the relationship?

"So we have answers of thirty-six and thirty-four." Carol writes the answers next to the problem. "Tamar, you got thirty-four. Why don't you start. How did you get thirty-four?"

"I added two to get to the other problem, one each time. So I took two more away and that made thirty-four." Tamar has noticed and made use of the prior problem, but he subtracts two, compensating.

"I did the same thing," Nikisha chimes in. "I noticed that it was one more there and one more there." She points to both numbers.

"So what happens to the answer?" Carol addresses the question to the whole class.

"It's the same," a few children respond. Tamar and Nikisha, who have taken two away and gotten thirty-four, look puzzled.

"So is it thirty-four or thirty-six?" Carol queries.

"Thirty-six," several other children respond.

"Shakina?" Carol broadens participation.

"This is what I did. I took away one from the seventy-five, and one from the thirty-nine, and I used Kashan's and Michael's rule not Tamar's rule. She points to a sign that Kashan and Michael had made some days before when they had invented this constant difference strategy. Their sign reads, "When you have a subtraction number sentence and you change both numbers the same way, then your answer will be the same. If you change only one number, or both numbers differently, your answer will not be the same. You can use this rule to help make some subtraction problems easier to solve." This

149

is a difficult strategy for children to understand, however, and not all the children have constructed an understanding of it.

"Tarique, do you still disagree? You took away two, so do you still think the answer is thirty-four?" Tarique still looks puzzled.

Jackie tries to prove that it is thirty-six by using a different strategy. "You could take away one hundred . . ."

Carol interrupts her. "Wait, let's talk about Tarique's thinking for a minute. He said he took away one from here and one from there and so you have to take away two more from the answer." Pointing to 139 and 175 on the number line from the previous problem, she asks, "What's the space in between, Tarique?"

"It's thirty-six."

Carol continues, "Okay, let's look at Tarique's thinking on the number line. Let's take one from here to 174 and one from here to 138 like you did (see Figure 8.23). How much is in between here? Nikisha?"

"Thirty-six."

"Why is it the same?"

"If you take one away to get 174 . . . it's like you're taking both numbers and just moving them down the same. So the difference is the same. They're both moving down one."

"Wow, that's a mouthful! Who understands what she is saying?" Carol asks for a paraphrase to give others a chance to think about it and to see how many children understand. Several hands are up, including Tarique's. "Tarique?"

"She said the distance is the same, because you are just taking one away from each, like if you took away two from 175 and only one from 139 . . . it would not be the same. She is saying that if you do the same to both numbers the distance is the same."

Carol now adds her own paraphrase. "Oh, the same *distance* on the

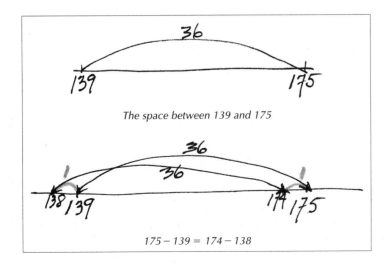

FIGURE 8.23
*Exploring "Constant
Difference" on the open
number line*

number line. Wow. So, Tarique, would it work if you move it up, say to 176 minus forty?"

"Yes, as long as both numbers move the same."

Tarique is now convinced that as long as the "distance" stays the same, the answers are the same. His understanding is now solid.

Canceling out Common Amounts

This last strategy was not on our original landscape as a landmark. Two boys in Carol's class, Tarique and Michael, invented it. The mathematics behind it is beautiful. Rather than explaining it, let's just watch it being invented. The problem under discussion is 120 − 109. Carol notices that Michael is thinking intently.

"Michael, do you have a question?"

"Well, I don't know if I'm right, but one hundred can't take away one hundred."

"What do you mean one hundred can't take away one hundred?" Carol is perplexed as to where he may be going.

"Well, it will be zero," Michael explains.

"One hundred take away one hundred is zero," Carol paraphrases, still perplexed. "How does that help? The answer to 120 minus 109 is not zero."

Tarique is shaking his head furiously. "No, the answer is eleven."

Carol brings him into the conversation. "Let's listen to Tarique for a minute."

"It's eleven, because, if you have a hundred and you take out a hundred that is zero."

"Okay." Carol is still puzzled as to what these boys are thinking.

Tarique goes on, "Now go up two more tens. That's 120. So it equals twenty, because the hundred minus a hundred equals zero. Starting from a hundred is really like starting from zero. So all we really have to do is take nine from twenty, and that is eleven."

"Does anyone understand?" Carol checks to see whether the other children are following Tarique's thinking. Almost everyone says no, but Jackie says that she thinks she understands at least a part of what he is saying. Carol asks her to try to explain.

"He is saying that one hundred minus one hundred equals zero . . . " Jackie pauses, a little unsure of what happens next. Several children start to interrupt her. Carol asks them to give Jackie some "think time." After a moment she continues, "Add nine to one hundred and twenty to the other hundred, and the difference is eleven."

"Is that what you're saying, Tarique? That all you have to look at is the twenty and the nine, because the hundreds cancel each other out?" Carol attempts to clarify. Tarique nods affirmatively.

If Tarique's strategy is represented on a double number line, a line can be drawn through both hundreds to show how they cancel each other out, leaving the simple problem of 20 − 9 (see Figure 8.24). This thinking is, of course, really constant difference. He has removed one hundred from each number. What is so nice about Tarique's thinking, though, is how he is able to see one hundred as another zero starting point. He eliminates the extraneous part of the problem. That's why he calls one hundred zero.

Represented algebraically, Tarique's thinking is $(a + b) - (a + c) = b - c$: a minus a just cancels out and we are left with a simple problem of $b - c$. Mathematicians often look for what can be canceled out. This is an important big idea in itself. Make a problem simpler by canceling out all equivalent amounts. Pare the problem down to its "bones."

This strategy might be useful in several instances. For example, in $108,002 - 100,008$, $100,000$ can be cancelled out, leaving a simple problem of $8,002 - 8$. Children who use the borrowing algorithm will make many mistakes because of all the borrowing needed and because of the zeroes. Children who have learned to look to the numbers first, who have a repertoire of strategies and a deep understanding of the big ideas involved, see relationships. They can simplify problems, play with numbers, and create. They choose a strategy that fits the problem. They *are* young mathematicians at work.

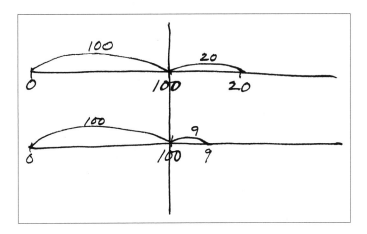

FIGURE 8.24
Tarique's strategy: canceling out the hundreds

SUMMING UP . . .

When René Descartes said, "Each problem that I solved became a rule which served afterwards to solve other problems," he said it all. When children are given the chance to compute in their own ways, to play with relationships and operations, they see themselves as mathematicians and their understanding deepens. Such playing with numbers forms the basis for algebra and will take children a long way in being able to compute not only efficiently but elegantly! As Max Dehn reminds us, "Mathematics is the only instructional material that can be presented in an entirely undogmatic way." Why has it taken us so long to realize it?

9 | ASSESSMENT

*If we do not change our direction,
we are likely to end up where we
are headed.*

— *Chinese Proverb*

The previous chapters have documented a great deal of teaching and learning. They are filled with stories of children and teachers hard at work: children, as they construct an understanding of our number system and of addition and subtraction; teachers, as they grapple with ways to facilitate this journey. The learning is evident in the conversations we have overheard and in the children's work. But is there a more formal way to assess it? And what is assessment, anyway? Is it the same thing as documentation or evaluation? And most important, what is its purpose or function?

Over the last forty years or so, answers to these questions have changed dramatically. For example, in 1967, Bloom and Foskay wrote,

> There is one field in which a considerable sophistication has developed since 1920: the field of achievement testing. It is possible now to study the degree and nature of a student's understanding of school subjects with a subtlety not previously available. Modern objective achievement tests, when properly developed and interpreted, offer one of the most powerful tools available for educational research. Findings have been made through their use that rise far above common sense. (65)

In the fifties, sixties, and seventies, teaching and learning were seen as two separate processes. Teachers taught by transmission and feedback; learners practiced and studied. It was believed that the knowledge that resulted could be measured in terms of behavioral outcomes. Taxonomies of behavioral objectives were developed, and curricula were written to match the desired outcomes. (See the hierarchical taxonomies of Gagné [1965]; Bloom et al. [1971]; and De Block [1975].) Content was broken down into skills and subskills, which were thought to accumulate into more encompassing concepts. Teachers were expected to focus all instruction toward these outcomes, and tests were designed to measure whether learners had "mastered" them (Bloom 1980).

The language used to discuss education during this period is interesting. *Skills* refers to skillful behavior, behavior that can be executed with skill. There is certainly skill involved in hammering nails or sawing wood. One can also type skillfully. But what do we mean when we talk about mathematical "skills"? Do skills constitute mathematical thinking, or did we begin to use that terminology because skills were outcomes that were easier to measure and because they refer to behavior? Certainly, if proficiency with an algorithm is the goal, one can talk of skills. But do "skills" with performing algorithms really get to the heart of mathematical *thinking*?

The term *concepts* is also grounded in behaviorism and the closely aligned psychology of associationism. One is said to have a concept of "fruit," for example, if it can be defined and associated with various exemplars—apples, peaches, and so on. Back then, we assessed concepts by whether or not learners could associate exemplars—another easily measurable outcome. In mathematics, we typically used the term *concept* to refer to topics like place value or addition. We measured outcomes by determining whether learners could associate ten bundled and two loose objects with the numeral 12, for example, or whether they could arrive at correct answers to addition problems. But is this term also a misnomer when one defines mathematics as mathematizing? Clearly, concepts do not equate to big ideas, nor do skills equate to strategies.

And *taxonomies,* by definition, categorize knowledge into a linear framework, not a landscape. Freudenthal objected to taxonomies because he saw them as a priori categories, postulated on logical grounds by designers of curricula, tests, and measurement tools (van den Heuvel-Panhuizen 1996). He argued that they were designed to categorize problems used in achievement tests rather than to represent the genuine development of knowledge coming from a post priori analysis of learners' work. To support his argument, he provided an example of how a taxonomy of outcomes that ascend in the order *knowledge, recognition, application, integration* could actually be found in the reverse when one looks at it from the development of the learner:

> Let us follow the pattern using the knowledge of 3 < 4; this is *integrated* by, for instance, comparing one's own family of three with the family of four next door; it is *applied* to other pairs of quantities; it is *recognized* by means of a one-to-one relationship ("because they have one more child"); and it becomes *knowledge* through the counting sequence 1, 2, 3, 4. . . . (cited in van den Heuvel-Panhuizen 1996, 22).

As outcomes became the focus, *what* we assessed and *how* we assessed it were determined by what was easy to assess and measure. By emphasizing the construction of the test items, it became easy to obtain a score and use this as a measure of evaluation. Assessment moved toward evaluation, because with these so-called objective, measurable outcomes we now had the ability to compare learners with one another, teachers with one another, and schools with one another. The function of assessment became evaluation—both of the individual and the group. The tests provided teachers with little or no information that could inform their teaching. Although they now had a score for a learner on an achievement test, this score provided no insights into the learner's developing abilities, strategies, conceptions, or ways of thinking. The scores were merely a quantitative way to compare learners with one another and to compare the number of correct answers with the total possible number of correct answers on a test. This ratio was assumed to be a score that reflected what students had learned.

Streefland (1981) has argued that assessment should be viewed not in the narrow sense of determining what the student has learned but from the standpoint of educational development—that it should provide teachers with information about what to teach. "Such reflective moments in education," he writes, "in which the teacher contemplates what has passed and what is still to come, are important" (35). But the direction in the sixties and seventies was away from such common sense, toward objective measurement. And what a path this has led us down!

Assessment outcomes today not only define what will be taught but also are used as gates to educational programs and schools. They are used to determine how much federal money schools will get. They put teachers on the line for job security and promotion. They are even used to evaluate schools and districts, thus affecting property values and the demography of neighborhoods. They are a high-stakes game. And make no mistake, they drive instruction.

PERFORMANCE-BASED ASSESSMENT

In the eighties and nineties, frameworks for teaching and learning began to shift. Emphasis was placed on learning as a constructive activity rather than as the result of transmission, practice, and reinforcement. As this new view of learning took hold, the inadequacies of the prevailing methods of assessment became apparent. In the words of Freudenthal, "We know that it is more informative to observe a student during his mathematical activity than to grade his papers" (1973, 84).

To meet the call for more "authentic" forms of assessment, tests were made up of open-ended tasks rather than closed questions with only one answer. These performance-based assessments were designed to evaluate students' activity, *how* they went about solving a problem, rather than their answers. For example, third graders might be asked to solve a problem like this:

> John was paid $2.50 for mowing the lawn and then went to the store to buy some chips. The chips cost 69 cents. He gave the cashier $1.00. How much change did he get back? How much money does he have now? Explain your thinking.

Notice two important aspects of this problem. First, there are no answers to choose from. Students must solve the problem in their own way. In that sense the problem is open. Second, students are asked to explain their thinking—to show their work and justify their answer. Opening up test items in such a way shifted assessment from isolated skills and concepts to something more holistic—mathematical activity in an authentic context. Responses were quantified by applying scoring rubrics.

This performance-based assessment, while a worthy attempt to analyze student thinking, brought with it a host of problems. First, a context meaningful in one culture may not be meaningful in another. (Mowing the lawn is a fact of life for a rural or suburban child, but a city child may never have seen a lawn.) Second, many of the assessment problems were written in prose and therefore depended on the learner's reading ability. Then too, second-language issues and writing facility affected learners' abilities to explain and justify their thinking. Were we assessing mathematical activity or language, culture, and writing ability? Given that the predominant use of these assessments was still evaluation of students, teachers, and schools, this was a serious issue.

PORTFOLIO-BASED DOCUMENTATION

Some researchers (for example, Pat Carini and Ted Chittendon, among others) stepped in and suggested that assessments focus on documentation of learning rather than evaluation. Portfolio assessment was one such alternative. Samples of children's work over time were placed in portfolios and used as evidence of children's capabilities. Teachers kept anecdotal records of their observations, interviewed their students, and wrote up their reflections. All materials were placed in the portfolio as evidence of the child's mathematical thinking. These portfolios obviously documented children's mathematical activity, but how did one describe and characterize the growth? Another set of questions arose. What made a good sample entry? What kind of rubric could be used to "score" a portfolio? Was there a way to standardize the outcomes so that they could be treated as objective measures—so that they could be used for evaluation? *Should* they be used for evaluation?

ASSESSING MATHEMATIZING

The shift to performance-based assessment and the use of portfolios was a change in direction toward assessing children's mathematizing, but rather than making the mathematizing visible, we seemed to be assessing how well children could explain their strategies. What does it mean to make mathematizing visible? What is the purpose of assessment when mathematics is defined as mathematizing?

Freudenthal argued that assessment should be meaningful and provide information that will benefit the connected act of teaching:

Examining is a meaningful activity. The teacher should be able to check the influence of the teaching process, at least in order to know how to improve it. The student has the right to know whether he has really learned something. . . . Finally there are others who are interested in knowing what somebody has learned. (1973, 83)

From this perspective, assessment needs to inform teaching. It needs "to foresee where and how one can anticipate that which is just coming into view in the distance" (Streefland 1985, 285). It needs to capture mathematizing, not the verbal prose explaining it. It needs to assess what the child can do, not what he can't do (De Lange 1992). It needs to capture where the child is on the landscape of learning—where she has been, what her struggles are, and where she is going. It must move from being static to being dynamic (van den Heuvel-Panhuizen 1996).

Assessment must be dynamic in the sense that it assesses *movement*—the journey. But it must also be dynamic by being *directly connected to learning and teaching*. If we teach in a way that supports mathematizing, then assessment must do the same. The information gleaned in assessment should directly inform and facilitate adjustments in teaching. For assessment to capture genuine mathematizing, for it to become dynamic, several criteria must be in place (van den Heuvel-Panhuizen 1996):

1. Students' own mathematical activity must be captured on the paper.
2. The test items must be meaningful and linked to reality.
3. Several levels of mathematizing must be possible for each item.
4. Assessment should inform teaching.

Capturing Genuine Mathematizing

There is a difference between writing about how you solved a problem and having the work visible. To capture actual work, provide scrap paper as part of the test (van den Heuvel-Panhuizen 1996). (See Figure 9.1 for an example.) Further, requiring students to use pens rather than pencils guarantees that all marks stay visible—nothing can be erased: different starts, changes in strategies, mistakes, rewriting, final figuring all get captured. Even with the bare sums in Figure 9.1, the scrap paper captures whether children add 25 + 26 by doing 25 + 25 + 1 or by doing 20 + 20 + 11 or by rewriting the problem vertically and doing an algorithm. For the third problem, do children proceed linearly or first arrange the numbers into friendly groups such as 10 + 15 + 15 = 10 + 30?

Linking Contexts to Reality

Contexts must allow children to mathematize—they must be more than word problems camouflaging "school mathematics." They must be real or be able to be imagined by children, just as the investigations used in teaching must be. One way to do this is to use pictures or tell stories. For example, by asking students to estimate the length of the limousine in Figure 9.2, students have to construct a unit of measurement, grounded in their reality. What is the approximate length of a window? Or the trunk? Or the distance of a seat?

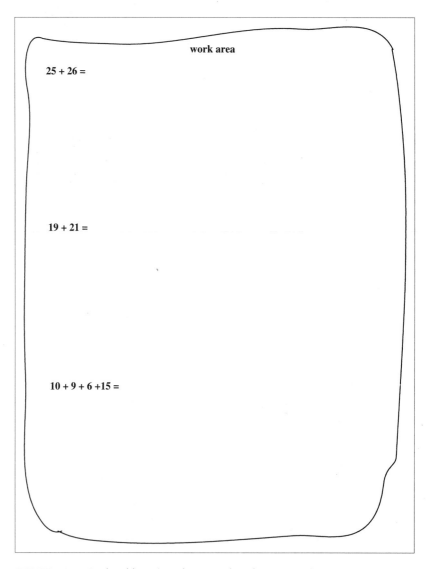

FIGURE 9.1   *Mixed problems (van den Heuvel-Panhuizen 1999)*

Providing for Various Levels of Mathematizing

The assessment items must be open enough that children can solve them in many ways. In the past, the test items themselves became progressively more difficult. One of the main problems with this approach is that "the students' behavior respects neither the taxonomies of objectives, nor the a priori analysis of difficulties" (Bodin 1993, 123). If we want to assess levels of mathematizing, then we need, instead, to open the tasks up and look at the *way* in which the answer to the question is found, not just *whether* the answer is found. For example, there are many ways to solve the "party" problem in

work area

A picture was taken of a giant limo.
 • **Make a reasonable estimation of the length of the real giant limo.**

FIGURE 9.2 *A giant limo (van den Heuvel-Panhuizen 1999)*

Figure 9.3. Children capable of a very high level of mathematizing would round 28 to 30 and 29 to 30 and immediately know that six trays of lemonade are needed. In contrast, some children may use tallies and then draw circles around groups of ten—a much lower level of mathematizing. The remainder will also be treated differently. Some children will treat it realistically: the people planning the party will need to order six trays. Others may treat the problem in a more "school mathematics" fashion, deriving an answer of 5 remainder 7.

Even items that assess students' number sense and mental math compu-

There are two classes in school that want to have a party. One class has 28 children. The other has 29.
 • How many of these trays are needed if every child gets one glass of lemonade?

FIGURE 9.3   *The class party (van den Heuvel-Panhuizen 1999)*

tation can allow levels of mathematizing. Take Figure 9.4, for example. On first glance, the items seem devoid of context. But the numbers in the problems have been chosen specifically because they can be treated differently. Children with good number sense are likely to solve the problem 71 − 36 as 70 − 35. Others may remove 40 and add back 4. Still others will need to

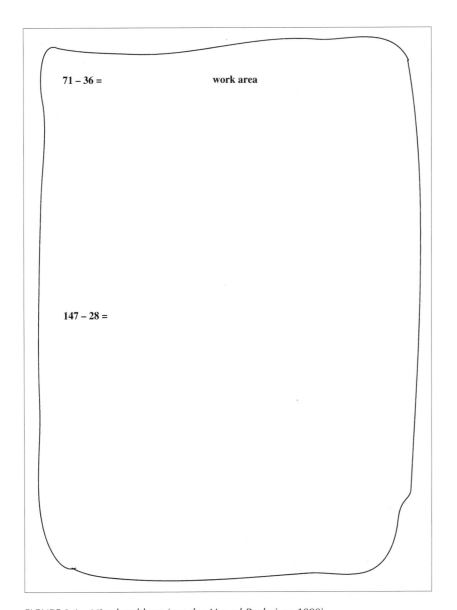

FIGURE 9.4   *Mixed problems (van den Heuvel-Panhuizen 1999)*

rewrite the problem vertically and perform a borrowing algorithm, treating each column as digits to cipher. Figure 9.5 illustrates four different levels of solutions to the problem $10 + 9 + 6 + 15$.

Informing Teaching

By assessing how a student mathematizes, teachers acquire information that enables them to determine how to proceed. They are able to understand where the child is within the landscape of learning. By analyzing the child's

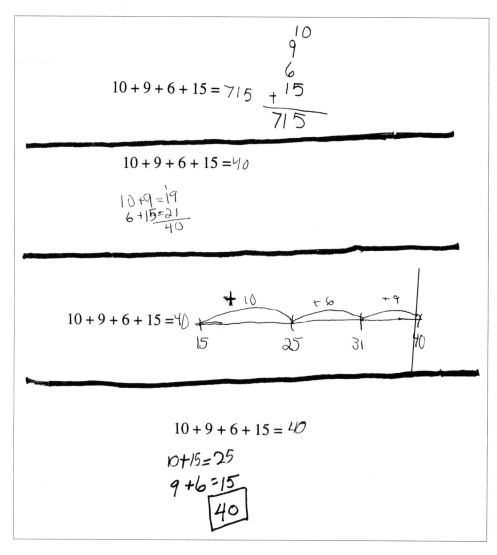

FIGURE 9.5   *Four different strategies to solve 10 + 9 + 6 + 15*

markings on the paper provided as part of the test, teachers are able to comprehend not only how the child is currently mathematizing but also what strategies she is trying out. The landscape of learning (which comprises strategies, big ideas, and models) informs the rubric used to analyze it but in turn also informs how it is taught. Because the landmarks become visible, teachers can determine appropriate horizons. In this way, learning and teaching are connected.

When the primary function of assessment is to inform teaching, evaluation is also redefined. Rather than "grading" schools and teachers with scores, we can characterize the mathematizing that is going on. We can evaluate the effect of various curricula and inservice professional development programs on this mathematizing. We can look at where the children are within the landscape of learning and describe where it is they need to go.

ASSESSMENT IN REFORMED CLASSROOMS

Assessing the Landscape of Learning

This book is built around a landscape of learning comprising the big ideas, strategies, and models related to early number sense and addition and subtraction (see Figure 9.6). When assessing young mathematicians in the classroom, it is the landmarks the students pass (collectively and severally) in their journey through this landscape that inform teachers' questions, instructional decisions, and the curriculum.

The landmarks in this journey toward numeracy are not necessarily sequential. Many paths can be taken toward this horizon. Some are, of course, precursors to others—one-to-one correspondence is a precursor to cardinality; cardinality is a precursor to unitizing. On the other hand, some children will develop computation strategies based on double plus or minus before they develop a strategy based on the making of tens; others, just the reverse. Some children will try out a strategy and only later construct the big idea that explains the strategy; others will construct the big idea first. Nor is this landscape definitive, or closed. Instead it represents what we have noticed so far in the journeys in our classrooms.

As in any real journey, new landmarks can appear, and new paths, uncharted before, can be carved out. The landscape included in this book is simply a representation of others' past journeys—it can inform teaching, but it can also be added to as teachers work with the young mathematicians in their classrooms. The landmarks are not a checklist or a list of behavioral outcomes. They are a means to focus on and describe students' mathematizing.

Assessing in the Moment

The best and perhaps most valid assessment happens while teaching and learning are going on. As students interact in the classroom (with the teacher and with other students), as situations are explored and mathematized, it is

FIGURE 9.6 *The landscape of learning: number sense, addition, and subtraction on the horizon showing land-mark strategies (rectangles), big ideas (ovals), and models (triangles).*

important to notice landmarks being passed. As the landscape becomes better understood, it is easier to observe, confer, and question in relation to important mathematical ideas, strategies, and models—to maximize mathematical teaching moments.

Anecdotal records document the journey, but they are also helpful reminders that can inform teaching. For example, Josephine, a first-grade teacher, documents Joachim's thinking, but her notes also remind her of where he is on the journey. She writes:

> I noticed that Joachim made a big leap today. He counted on today when he was playing a board game with Michael. Always before when he would throw two dice to determine how many steps to move, he would count all the dots on the dice. Today I gave him one die with numerals, and the other with dots, in the hope that they would encourage him to count on. I noticed that when he rolled a numeral six on one die and five dots on the other, that he said, "Six . . . 7, 8, 9, 10, 11." He continued to do this throughout the game. Tomorrow perhaps I'll give him two numeral dice. This may be too big a leap, but I'll see what he does.

Josephine has documented a particular moment of Joachim's journey. Her observation also informs her teaching. The note records her instructional choice on this day and reminds her that tomorrow she wants to encourage Joachim to continue to count on.

Portfolio Assessment

Students and teachers can choose samples of work for a mathematics portfolio. Dates can be stamped on each piece and notes can be added in relation to the landscape. The notes both document learning over time and inform teaching. For example, teacher Susannah Blum might discuss Josie's work on the seed problem (see Figure 9.7) with her, and together they might note how Josie knew that three boxes would be 300 seeds and how she had represented each hundred with ten packages. The work depicts Josie's journey toward unitizing—an important landmark. Over the course of the year, Josie's portfolio will swell with evidence of her mathematizing—and of her development as a young mathematician.

Paper-and-Pencil Assessments

As long as the test items are designed in relation to the criteria described in this chapter, paper-and-pencil tests can provide important information. Notes about how children solve $49 + 47$ or $10 + 9 + 6 + 15$ on their scrap paper can indicate whether children are making use of number relationships as they calculate. For example, $49 + 47$ can be solved by regrouping the numbers as $50 + 50 - 4$ or $50 + 46$. On the other hand, some children may need to take smaller leaps: $49 + 40 + 1 + 6$ or even $49 + 10 + 10 + 10$

+ 10 + 1 + 6. Still others may not use relationships at all but rewrite the problem vertically and perform the algorithm. Some children will solve 10 + 9 + 6 + 15 using number relationships—10 + 15 + 15 = 10 + 30 or 25 + 15. Others will work only in linear order. Still others will need to rewrite it in order to perform the algorithm.

ASSESSMENT RESULTS: MAKING THE LANDSCAPE VISIBLE

How do children in classrooms like those depicted in this book compare with children in traditional classrooms, in which mathematics is taught as procedures? To look at this question, an assessment with items that were open enough to capture various levels of mathematizing was designed (van den Heuvel-Panhuizen 1999). It was given to third graders in classrooms in which the Mathematics in the City program was being well implemented. It was also given to third graders in classrooms in the same schools or district in which algorithms were taught and little attempt was made to engage chil-

FIGURE 9.7   *Josie's work: evidence of unitizing*

dren in mathematizing. Responses were coded with a rubric that reflected the landscape of learning.

The children's answers were not significantly different; however, their position within the landscape of learning differed remarkably (van den Heuvel-Panhuizen 2000). Children in classrooms in which number relationships and context were emphasized outperformed their traditionally taught peers significantly in using strategies representative of number sense. They easily composed and decomposed numbers to make them friendly, frequently computing mentally. Traditionally taught children relied on algorithms no matter what the numbers were. Children in reformed classrooms treated answers to problems within the context. For example, when asked to figure out how many trays of lemonade were needed for a class party (see Figure 9.3), most of these children responded, "Six trays," whereas many of the traditionally taught children either needed to perform the algorithm, ending up with a remainder, or performed the wrong operation.

STANDARDIZED TEST RESULTS

Unfortunately most school districts are still held accountable on state and city standardized tests. In New York City, this test is the Terra Nova. It is a multiple-choice, standardized achievement test similar to those used by most school districts. We again compared third graders based on the results of this test and found a difference significant at the .0001 level: Mathematics in the City third graders (n = 562) outperformed the control group (n = 2,200). It is particularly interesting that Mathematics in the City third graders did significantly better on all of the subtests related to number.

We share these results not because we believe standardized tests are the best way to assess learning. We don't, and we have tried to make that clear in this chapter. It is often argued, however, that change cannot occur in light of the pressure brought to bear because standardized assessments are used. Many districts mandate that teachers teach to the test. Pacing calendars aligned with the standardized tests determine curriculum in these districts and direct instruction, practice, and test preparation characterize these classrooms. When this happens, assessment drives instruction and children are taught only the kind of thinking that can easily be assessed by these tests. They are not taught to think, to mathematize. Our data are proof that the practice of teaching to the test is a misappropriation of time. If children are taught in a way that allows them to construct understanding, they will perform better, even on standardized tests.

SUMMING UP . . .

The Chinese proverb used as the epigraph to this chapter states, "If we do not change our direction, we are likely to end up where we are headed." If we teach directly to standardized achievement tests, we may end up with children who can pass them but who know little mathematics. If we want to encourage mathematizing and the development of number relationships, we need to teach in a way that supports it.

Early attempts at assessment were driven by learning based on behaviorism and the belief that tests could measure this learning objectively. As our understanding of learning shifted to include a deeper analysis of cognitive development, one characterized by constructivism, these tests were seen as insufficient. Performance-based assessment and portfolios replaced earlier tests. Problems arose, however, over whether we were assessing language or mathematics and how to quantify scores on portfolios.

Assessments need to inform teaching, and they need to reflect mathematizing. If assessments are developed that make mathematizing visible and include realistic items that can be mathematized on many levels, they can be beneficial. They can document the journey toward the horizon of numeracy. The landscape of learning can serve as a framework, since it depicts important landmarks. However, these landmarks are not a list of outcomes but a representation of many past journeys.

When young mathematicians are hard at work, they are thinking, they become puzzled, they become intrigued; they are learning to see their world through a mathematical lens. Assessment needs to capture the view this lens reveals.

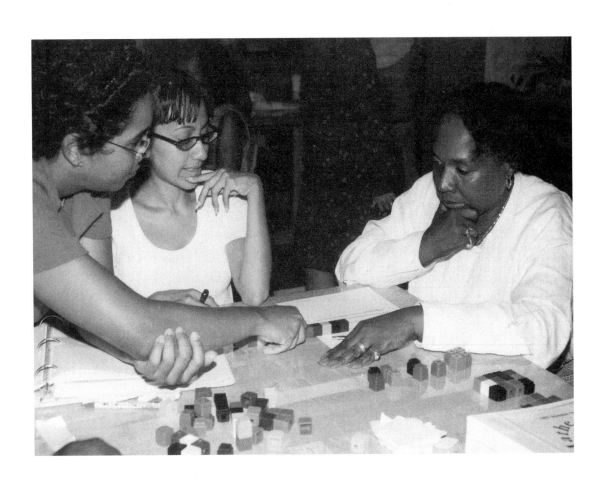

10 | TEACHERS AS MATHEMATICIANS

Life is good for only two things, discovering mathematics and teaching mathematics.

— *Siméon Poisson, quoted in* Mathematics Magazine

Gel'fand amazed me by talking of mathematics as though it were poetry. He once said about a long paper bristling with formulas that it contained the vague beginnings of an idea which he could only hint at, and which he had never managed to bring out more clearly. I had always thought of mathematics as being much more straightforward: a formula is a formula, and an algebra is an algebra, but Gel'fand found hedgehogs lurking in the rows of his spectral sequences!

—*Dusa McDuff in* Mathematical Notices

So far this book has focused on *young* mathematicians—children between the ages of four and eight hard at work constructing, questioning, mathematizing, and communicating their world through a mathematical lens. But if teachers are to be able to facilitate mathematical journeys for the young learners with whom they work, they need to have a strong understanding of the subject as well. In the United States, teacher education programs have added more and more mathematics courses. Over the last ten years, in fact, there has been an impetus to make a liberal arts undergraduate degree a requirement for teacher certification. Usually this has meant that education programs have been reduced to a single year (thirty credits) so that a bachelor of arts degree can still be obtained in four years or a master of arts in five. In essence, the trend has been to increase the length of the overall program, increase the number of liberal arts courses, and decrease the number of education courses. Today, teachers in the United States are required to take more college mathematics courses than ever before, yet the gap between the needed and the actual content understanding seems to be widening. The cry for in-service professional development has become a roar. Why are our teachers so ill prepared?

Some critics blame the teachers. They push for stricter entrance requirements for teacher education programs—higher grade-point averages and better scores on entrance examinations. Many states have developed their own examinations and introduced tiered certifications—initial, provisional, permanent, professional. A master's degree is often required to receive a permanent license, and salaries have been raised. All of these reforms have produced little real change in teachers' competence in mathematics.

Teacher educators in the Netherlands have taken a different tack. People who want to become primary school teachers in the Netherlands do not attend a university, pursue a liberal arts degree, or take courses in a mathematics department. Instead, they attend *Hogeschool,* a four-year post–high school program specifically focused on teacher preparation. During the four years, students take some seven or eight courses in mathematics education, courses geared toward a deep understanding of the mathematical topics *they will be teaching.* Prospective teachers learn about the big ideas embedded in the topics, about how children's strategies develop, about important mathematical models. They learn about the role of context and how to use didactical models like the open number line. They explore number patterns and mental math strategies. They become strong mathematical thinkers *in relation to the topics they will be teaching*—the landscape they will journey through with their children. But is this even enough?

Korthagen and Kessel (1999) have argued that a major problem with teacher education programs is that they are grounded in theory and methods, in *episteme,* and what is taught does not transfer to the classroom. Prospective teachers have preconceptions about learning and teaching that come from their past experiences as students. These preconceptions are so strong they prove resistant to new learning, particularly when the new learning is divorced from practice. It's true that most teacher decision making is split second and grounded in perception, feelings, interpretation, and reaction (Dolk 1997). Teachers respond based on their subconscious beliefs about teaching and learning and on their overall vision of practice—beliefs and a vision developed during many years of being learners themselves, most often in classrooms in which mathematics was defined as a discipline to be transmitted.

Teachers who are already in the classroom are rarely different. Although they have more experience, their belief systems often are not aligned with the belief systems implicit in the new curricula or in education reform. John is typical. Asked about his beliefs about teaching he says, "How do I view the process of teaching? Part actor, part salesman. You have this body of knowledge that you have to get across to kids, but most students really don't want to be in school, so you have to sell them on this education kick. If you don't make your presentation good and you're not a good actor, they're not going to buy" (Fosnot 1993). Unless these beliefs are challenged and modified, when John is given new curricula based on constructivism, he will assume that the purpose of problem solving is to motivate children. He will see activity as important to promote interest. He will adopt new pedagogical strategies, but he will see them as new strategies to help him "get the body of knowledge across."

How do we help teachers (both preservice and inservice) develop a new conception of the nature of mathematics, one based on the human activity of making meaning through a mathematical lens? How do we revise the picture of what should be happening in the classroom? These two questions get at the heart of what is required in teacher education if reform is to be successful. Providing teachers with new textbooks or new pedagogical strategies will produce only superficial changes. The new strategies will be implemented within the constructs of the belief systems teachers already hold.

To get John and those like him to analyze and reflect on their beliefs, teacher education itself must undergo radical change. It needs to be grounded in new visions of practice based on how students learn. This often means creating disequilibrium with regard to prior conceptions. Rather than basing our work with teachers on *episteme*, we need to look to a framework based on *phronesis* and *constructivism* (Fosnot 1989, 1993, 1996; Korthagen and Kessel 1999). *Phronesis* is situation-specific knowledge related to the context in which it is used—in this case, the processes of teaching and learning. Constructivism describes learning as the process of building one's own understanding by modifying prior schemes and structures. Rather than teaching teachers about theory, which we then expect them to apply, we need to give them experiences that involve action, reflection, and conversation within the context of teaching and learning. They need to construct new beliefs, a new vision of what it means to teach and learn mathematics. They need to experience an environment in which mathematics is taught as mathematizing and learning is seen as constructing.

When teachers themselves model situations mathematically, construct solutions, set up relationships, and defend their ideas to their peers, their vision of mathematics pedagogy and their definition of mathematics begin to shift. By reflecting on their own learning and what facilitated it, they begin to form new beliefs—ones that often contradict prior beliefs. These in turn will become the basis for the way in which they react, question, and interact during learning/teaching moments. Teachers also need more situation-specific knowledge that can inform their decision making—more knowledge about how children develop mathematical ideas and strategies, a better ability to see and understand the mathematics in children's work. They need to understand mathematics as the human activity of mathematizing. And they need to understand the landscape of learning.

Throughout this book we have shown you teachers who define mathematics as mathematizing, who value their children's mathematical ideas and strategies, who promote genuine mathematical discourse within a community of mathematicians. These teachers walk the edge between the structure of mathematics and student development, between the individual and the community. In fact, they are willing to *live* on the edge, not always knowing the direction the path will take, to challenge themselves mathematically. They have acquired an in-depth understanding of the mathematical topics they teach and of the landscape of learning—the big ideas, the strategies, and the models. But they have done more. They have come to see themselves as mathematicians, to understand that mathematics is the human activity of mathematizing. They have learned to mathematize their world.

LEARNING TO MATHEMATIZE

Once again, the most vivid way for us to illustrate what we mean is to invite you into a teacher education session as the participants grapple with some mathematical ideas and then reflect on their learning and teaching.

Exploring the Edge

The participants in a Mathematics in the City professional development workshop are discussing numbers of beads (in two colors) that will make perfect patterned necklaces (a context similar to "Grandma's necklace," the activity Madeline Chang's students were exploring in Chapter 1). The challenge has been broadened to include not only patterns of alternating fives but also fours and threes, and the participants are trying to come up with a rule that will apply to any size alternating groups.

Opening up the context to include any size group makes it possible for the participants to investigate the context much more deeply, to construct algebraic expressions and representations if they wish, and to raise and explore additional questions (what if there were three colors instead of two?). Broadening the investigation in this way raises the difficulty level substantially and allows teachers to work on their mathematical edge, being learners in a mathematical environment.

The participants have discussed how some quantities work perfectly (like twenty in alternating groups of five, or sixteen in alternating groups of four). They have defined these as "perfect" necklaces, as opposed to "flawed" necklaces in which the pattern includes a partial grouping (sixteen beads arranged in alternating groups of five, for example, would have a single bead separating the pattern) or necklaces in which the pattern is broken entirely (twenty-one beads in alternating groups of five would include one group of six).

Clarissa, a first-grade teacher, is explaining her thinking to Mary, another first-grade teacher. "Well, I can see lots of numbers that work perfectly . . . if your pattern is five, two times five works, four times five, six times five. And if your pattern is four, it's the same . . . two times four, four times four, six times four, eight times four." On a large piece of paper, Clarissa and Mary have made two columns, which they have labeled *Works* and *Doesn't Work* (see Figure 10.1). Clarissa continues filling in the *Works* column. "Same with threes, two times three works, four times three . . . "

"So it seems there's a pattern," Mary comments. "It doesn't matter what the size of the group is . . . it's always two times it, then four times it, then six . . . it's every other number . . . two, four, six, eight, ten, and it will keep going like that."

"Yeah, but what about numbers that don't work? That seems harder."
Clarissa shifts to the other column.

"Well, we know twenty-one doesn't work because we all tried that one,"
Mary offers. (Cathy had used this amount to demonstrate a number that
didn't work when she was introducing the context.) "And twenty-five, because you would get ten of the same color in a row."

Works	doesn't work
(5's)	
2 x5=10	21
4 x5=20	25
6 x5=30	31
8 x5=40	35
10 x5=50	
(4's)	
2 x4=8	12
4 x4=16	20
6 x4=24	28
8 x4=32	36
10 x4=40	
(3's)	
2 x3=6	3 x3 =9
4 x3=12	4 x3+1 = 13
6 x3=18	5 x3 =15
8 x3=24	6 x3+1 = 19
10 x3=30	6 x3+2 = 20

FIGURE 10.1   *Mary's and Clarissa's chart*

"Right," Clarissa agrees. "So then thirty-one and thirty-five won't work either."

Although Mary and Clarissa are intrigued with the patterns they are noticing and are using them to generate further numbers, they are not exploring why the patterns are happening, which keeps them from being able to generalize. This is often the case in investigations. Patterns intrigue learners, and they use them. Often they assume a pattern will continue even though they have seen it in a limited number of examples. To really understand the pattern, to generalize beyond the examples (in other words, to really do mathematics), the relationships in the pattern must be defined and quantified. However, noticing patterns is often the beginning of a good mathematical question—one that leads mathematicians to consider why patterns are happening and whether they will always happen in that specifically defined situation. As Mary and Clarissa continue, they notice and make use of several patterns.

Mary puts forth a conjecture. "If even numbers of groups work, then let's try odds . . . the ones in between. They shouldn't work. Three times four, five times four, seven times four . . . none of these work."

As they continue collecting data and recording the information on their chart, their thinking shifts and then integrates. First they add tens, as they record twenty-one and twenty-five, then thirty-one and thirty-five. When they explore the fours, they shift to odd groups. When they move to the threes, they begin to integrate both these strategies, but still not systematically.

"So we know three groups of three won't work, because two groups of three did." Clarissa adds 9 to the chart.

"Right, and if we add one to four groups of three, we get thirteen. That won't work either," Mary continues.

They write 13 on the chart and continue filling in odd numbers of groups and even numbers of groups plus one, producing 15 and 19. Here their strategy shifts. They try an even number of threes plus two, producing 20. Eileen and Amy are sitting nearby. Eileen notices that although Clarissa and Mary have worked on necklaces with fours and threes, they only have four numbers on their chart that don't work for necklaces made with groups of five—21, 25, 31, 35.'

"There's more than those that don't work." Eileen points to the 21, 25, 31, 35 written on Clarissa and Mary's chart. "See, we found all of these, too."

Eileen and Amy have written a rule on their chart: *Take the first number that works perfectly and add each digit up to the number you're making the pattern with. Ten works with a five pattern, so add 1, 2, 3, 4, or 5 to find numbers that don't work (11, 12, 13, 14, 15 do not work).* At the bottom of the chart they have written, *All other numbers between perfect and not working at all make imperfect necklaces.* They have also noticed that multiplying two times the number in the pattern and adding this amount each time makes perfect necklaces.

Although Eileen and Amy have attempted to generalize, the language they use ("Take the *first* number that works . . .") does not depict their meaning. (The first number in this case is 10.) Then they go on to define the numbers that don't work as numbers that are produced when 1, 2, 3, 4, or 5 are added to it. They are trying to generalize, but their use of the word *first* produces only five specific numbers that don't work, rather than the general case of all numbers that don't work. The problem is compounded when they conclude that numbers between the perfect ones and the ones that don't work at all are the imperfect ones. Using this definition, that would be numbers between 10 and 11!

Language is critical in mathematics. In order to use algebraic symbols to represent the relationships, one has to be very clear what the relationships are. Lewis Carroll's books illustrate this so well. In *Alice's Adventures in Wonderland* he writes:

> "Then you should say what you mean," the March Hare went on.
> "I do," Alice hastily replied, "at least I mean what I say, that's the same thing, you know."
> "Not the same thing a bit!" said the Hatter. "Why, you might just as well say that 'I see what I eat' is the same thing as 'I eat what I see'!"

And in *Through the Looking Glass*, Humpty Dumpty and Alice have a similar debate:

> "When I use a word," Humpty Dumpty said, in a rather scornful tone, "it means just what I choose it to mean—neither more nor less."
> "The question is," said Alice, "whether you can make words mean so many different things."

In algebra, one symbol (*x*, for example) does mean many things. That's why we call it a variable. But when we set up an equation with these symbols, the *relationships* represented are specific. The *definition* of the variable is also specific. The mathematician Lichtenberg expressed this power of algebraic language well when he wrote, "In mathematical analysis we call *x* the undetermined part of line *a*: the rest we don't call *y*, as we do in common life, but *a − x*. Hence mathematical language has great advantages over the common language" (Woodard 2000). The symbols used in algebra are defined *in relationship to* one another. And this gets right to the heart of mathematics—the describing and quantifying of relationships. Amy and Eileen, as well as several other participants, are struggling to do this—to describe the relationships they are noticing.

Danielle and Steve, working at another table, are dealing with the same dilemma—how to write down specifically what they mean. On their paper they have written: *Any odd number of repetitions of the pattern will* not *work*.

"There's got to be a way to write this clearly so people will understand what we mean," Steve says.

"Well, we know that if we add numbers to that it becomes flawed . . . up to five; and when the necklace is made with groups of four, you stop at four; and with threes, three." Danielle gives examples of their findings and then concludes, "So up to the number in the group. Like if the necklace is made with three beads of one color, then you add numbers up to the amount in the group."

"Oh, that's good. Let's write that." Steve writes: *Add any numbers up to "y," where* y = *the number of beads in the pattern. This will produce a flawed necklace.*

Although Danielle and Steve state that "up to y" will be flawed, this of course is not true. When you add *y* to an odd number of groups, you get an even number of groups, and that is a perfect necklace. Nevertheless, Danielle and Steve are trying hard to define their ideas using a variable, and to describe the relationship of the amount added to the amount in the group. They go on to write: *Any even number of repetitions of "y" will work perfectly, and if we add any number up to "y" to that, it no longer works.*

Danielle begins to get excited. "So if the perfect necklaces are even numbers of groups, then it's two times any number. That makes an even number. Two *n*. So two *n* times the number of beads in the group, call that *p* . . . for pattern . . . makes a perfect necklace." She ends with a flourish and writes: (2n)p = *the perfect necklace.* "Wow, this is exciting . . . we're awesome!"

Frieda, Joan, and Nancy, who are working nearby, overhear. They have also grappled with an algebraic representation but have defined their terms differently. They see two times the number in the group as the unit and have written the following expression for the flawed necklace: (2n)x − *any number less than* n, *where* n = *the number of beads in the group.* They share this with Danielle and Steve. But now there is confusion over what *n* stands for, since the two groups are defining it differently. Danielle and Steve define *n* as "any whole number," thus 2*n* is any even number. Frieda, Joan, and Nancy define *n* as the number of beads in the group, so 2*n* to them is the number of beads in two groups, or one larger group comprising both colors. Their *n* is analogous to Danielle and Steve's *p*.

"Oh . . . my head hurts trying to think about this," Frieda comments with a sigh but nevertheless still intrigued. "I haven't thought this hard about math in a long, long time . . ."

So often we take for granted that because teachers have had algebra courses and can manipulate algebraic equations, their understanding is solid. But so much of the mathematics that teachers have learned in their past schooling is procedural; almost never have they been asked to *construct* mathematics. Further, the procedures they learned were taught by explanation. Often even the basic pre-algebraic ideas are not really understood.

Algebra was invented because mathematicians needed to communicate their ideas to one another—to communicate the relationships they noticed. Algebraic symbols can be used in many ways, and mathematicians decide for themselves what relationships to express and how to express them. For teachers to appreciate the feelings of empowerment that come from building an idea for oneself, and to become able to generate the same feelings in their students, they must experience the process. They must learn what it means to work on the edge, to challenge themselves mathematically, to think hard. They must learn that puzzlement is an important process in learning. (Einstein once said, "Do not worry about your difficulties in mathematics, I assure you that mine are greater"!) Teachers must be willing to see themselves as mathematicians and to understand that mathematics is a creative process—one that often demands a struggle. Only then will they really understand the exhilaration and empowerment that comes from doing mathematics—from constructing and mathematizing their world.

Living in a Mathematical World

Being a mathematician means thinking about mathematics outside the classroom as well as in it. It means being willing to work on problems at home, to wonder about them during your commute to work, to raise your own mathematical inquiries. Toward this end, we ask teachers in our workshops and courses to keep double-entry journals. On one side they are to continue the mathematics they have been doing during the day—reflect on other participants' mathematical ideas, do more work on ideas they did not fully understand, raise other questions and/or mathematical inquiries. (We often form inquiry groups around these mathematical questions and pursue them during the institutes.) The other side of the journal is for recording insights about learning and teaching—what enabled them to learn the things they learned, what strategies they might try in their classrooms to help children learn. These pedagogical insights should be connected to the insights related to their own learning: that's why it's a *double*-entry journal. Our aim is to give teachers new beliefs, a new vision of practice, and then help them transform these beliefs into practical strategies—to ground teacher education in an analysis of the connection between learning and teaching.

After the class we previously described, Frieda wrote in the mathematics side of her journal:

> I have to be honest, I didn't really understand what n was in the equations. I still don't, so . . .
>
> Two times any number? Times p? I see that p is the number in the pattern (four, for example), or . . . is it the number of the complete pattern? Maybe n is the number of the set used as the pattern? If we do 2 times the number of the set, then it is always perfect (because there are two colors), so p could be any number. That's interesting. But if we make p the number of complete patterns and multiply the $2n$ times that, then that gives us the total number of beads used . . . and of course the pattern will be perfect. Hmmm . . .

Frieda then draws partial arrays that look like portions of a hundreds chart (see Figure 10.2). These arrays are models of the situation, but they are also models Freida is using as tools to think with. She represents two situations: necklaces made with groups of five, and necklaces made with groups of three. For five she draws an array that has 10, 20, 30, and 40 at the right. She labels these the perfect ones. The others in the array are the imperfect ones. She also draws the complete pattern, two sets of fives, each a different color— $2n$. She goes on to explain how p can be any number because of the repeated addition. Then she formulates a new solution:

> So if I take the total number of beads and divide it by the number of beads in the group, I should get an even number. If I get an even number, it's a perfect necklace! If I get an odd number, it's a necklace that doesn't work! If the total number of beads divided by the number of beads in the pattern is odd with a remainder, it will be an imperfect necklace. If it is even with a remainder, the necklace doesn't work!

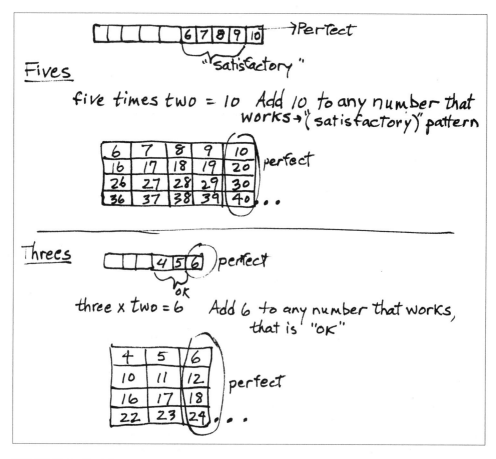

FIGURE 10.2   *Partial arrays*

Not only has Frieda worked out what *n* represents, she has built an elegant, efficient solution!

Then, on the pedagogical side of her double-entry journal, Frieda reflects on how her own learning will affect her teaching:

> I discovered that I was able to think mathematically, although it was difficult. Everyone can arrive at answers, but maybe through different means. Investigating problems and looking for patterns was essential. I want to make math part of everyday reality and stretch kids from where they are . . .

Danielle also wrote down some reflections that evening:

> I was fascinated to discover that generalizations lead to other generalizations. [Learning] seems to work like concentric circles. First we made a generalization for patterns of five. Then we realized it would work for patterns of any number. Then we realized that the conjecture (is that what I mean by generalization?) applied to odd and even repetitions of the pattern with two colors. . . . Now I'm wondering what happens when you have a three-color pattern instead of two. What is the relationship between the number of colors in the pattern and the number of repetitions of the pattern? And I'll never ever think of a beaded necklace in the same way again. Now I'll look at necklaces and start to think about the algebra of the pattern!

Danielle and Frieda are beginning to see themselves as mathematicians. They are willing to raise and pursue mathematical inquiries—to see the world through a mathematical lens. They are enjoying and appreciating the puzzlement that accompanies genuine learning, taking pleasure in "creating and figuring out."

SUMMING UP . . .

For teachers to be able to teach in the ways illustrated in these chapters, they need to walk the edge between the structure of mathematics and child development, between the community and the individual. They need to be willing to live on the edge. They need to be willing to challenge themselves mathematically and to be willing to journey with their children. There is no one path, one line, one map for the journey. The landscape of learning has many paths, and the horizons shift as we approach them. Knowing the landscape, having a sense of the landmarks—the big ideas, the strategies, and the models—helps us plan the journey. We need to structure the environment to bring children closer to the landmarks, to the horizon—to enable them to act on their world mathematically.

Just as mathematics learning needs to be situated in context, in the environment of the landscape, teacher education needs to be situated in the context of teaching/learning. New belief systems and a new vision of practice need to be constructed through subsequent reflection on learning and teaching. Teachers need to see themselves as mathematicians. If we foster environments in which teachers can begin to see mathematics as mathematizing—as constructing mathematical meaning in their lived world—they will be better able to facilitate the journey for the young mathematicians with whom they work.

REFERENCES

BEISHUIZEN, M., K. P. E. GRAVEMEIJER, and E. C. D. M. VAN LIESHOUT. 1997. *The Role of Contexts and Models in the Development of Mathematical Strategies and Procedures.* Utrecht: Utrecht University (CD-β series on research in education; 26).

BEMELMANS, L. 1977. *Madeline.* New York: Viking Press.

BLOOM, B. S. 1980. *All Our Children Learning.* New York: McGraw-Hill.

BLOOM, B. S., and A. W. FOSKAY. 1967. "Formulation of hypotheses." In *International Study of Achievement in Mathematics: A Comparison in Twelve Countries,* ed. T. Huson, I, 64–76. Stockholm: Almqvist and Wiskell.

BLOOM, B. S., J. T. HASTINGS, and G. F. MADAUS. 1971. *Handbook on Formative and Summative Evaluation of Student Learning.* New York: McGraw-Hill.

BLUM, S. 1999. "Seed Time." Unpublished paper, City College of the City University of New York.

BODIN, A. 1993. "What does 'to assess' mean? The case of assessing mathematical knowledge." In *Investigations into Assessment in Mathematics Education,* ed. M. Niss, 113–41. Dordrecht: Kluwer.

CAMERON, A., and D. JACKSON. 1998. "Analyzing the Role of Teachers' Questions." Unpublished manuscript, City College of the City University of New York.

CARROLL, L. [1872] 1940. *Through the Looking Glass.* Reprint, Mt. Vernon, N.Y.: Peter Pauper Press.

CARROLL, L. [1865] 1946. *Alice's Adventures in Wonderland.* Reprint, New York: Grosset and Dunlop.

COBB, P. 1987. "Information-processing psychology and mathematics education—a constructivist perspective." *The Journal of Mathematical Behavior* 6(1), 4–40.

COBB, P. 1997. "Instructional design and reform: a plea for developmental research in context." In *The Role of Contexts and Models in the Development of Mathematical Strategies and Procedures,* eds. M. Beishuizen,

K. P. E. Gravemeijer, and E. C. D. M. van Lieshout, 273–89. Utrecht: Utrecht University (CD-β series on research in education; 26).

DANTZIG, T. 1930, 1959. *Number, The Language of Science.* New York: Macmillan.

DE BLOCK, A. 1975. *Taxonomy of Instructional Objectives.* Antwerp. Cited by van den Heuvel-Panhuizen, M. (1996).

DEHN, M. 1983. Quoted in A. Shenitzer (translator), Max Dehn. "The mentality of the mathematician: a characterization." *The Mathematical Intelligencer* 5(2), 18–26.

DE LANGE, J. 1992. "Critical factors for real changes in mathematics learning." In *Assessment and Learning of Mathematics,* ed. G. C. Leder, 305–329. Hawthorn, Victoria: Australian Council for Educational Research.

DESCARTES, R. 1637. *Discours de la méthode pour bien conduire sa raison & chercher la varité dans les sciences plus la diotrique, les meteores, et la geometrie, qui sont des essais de cette methode.* Leyde: I. Maire.

DOLK, M. 1997. *Onmiddellijk onderwijsgedrag over denken en handelen van leraren in onmiddellijke onderwijssituaties.* Utrecht: W.C.C.

DUCKWORTH, E. 1987. *The Having of Wonderful Ideas & Other Essays on Teaching and Learning.* New York: Teachers College Press.

EDDINGTON, SIR ARTHUR (1882–1944), quoted in N. Rose. 1988. *Mathematical Maxims and Minims.* Raleigh, NC: Rome Press.

EVES, H. W. 1972. *Mathematical Circles Squared.* Boston: Prindle, Weber and Schmidt.

FOSNOT, C. T. 1989. *Enquiring Teachers, Enquiring Learners.* New York: Teachers College Press.

FOSNOT, C. T. 1993. "Learning to teach, teaching to learn: the center for constructivist teaching/teacher preparation project." *Teaching Education* 5(2), 69–78.

FOSNOT, C. T., ed. 1996. *Constructivism: Theory, Perspectives, and Practice.* New York: Teachers College Press.

FREUDENTHAL, H. 1968. "Why to Teach Mathematics so as to Be Useful." *Educational Studies in Mathematics* I, 3–8.

FREUDENTHAL, H. 1973. *Mathematics as an educational task.* Dordrecht: Reidel.

FREUDENTHAL, H. 1975. "Pupils' Achievements Internationally Compared—the IEA." *Educational Studies in Mathematics,* 6, 127–86.

FREUDENTHAL, H. 1991. *Revisiting Mathematics Education. The China Lectures.* Dordrecht: Kluwer.

GAGNÉ, R. 1965. *The Conditions of Learning.* London: Holt, Rinehart, and Winston.

GAUSS, K. F. (1777–1855). 1808 Letter to Bolyai.

GRAVEMEIJER, K. P. E. 1991. "An instruction-theoretical reflection on the use of manipulatives." In *Realistic Mathematics Education in Primary School,* ed. L. Streefland. Utrecht: Utrecht University (CD-β series on research in education; 9).

GRAVEMEIJER, K. P. E. 1999. "How emergent models may foster the constitution of formal mathematics." *Mathematical Thinking and Learning* I(2), 155–77.

GRAVEMEIJER, K. P. E. 2000. "A local instruction theory on measuring and flexible arithmetic." Paper presented at the International Conference of Mathematics Educators, Tokyo, Japan. August.

GUEDJ, D. 1996. *Numbers: The Universal Language.* Paris: Gallimard. English translation (1997). New York: Harry Abrams.

HANLON, G. 1996. Unpublished journal. Personal communication.

HARDY, G. H. 1941. *A Mathematician's Apology:* London: Cambridge University Press.

HERSH, R. 1997. *What Is Mathematics, Really?* London: Oxford University Press.

HUGHES, M. 1986. *Children and Number: Difficulties in Learning Mathematics.* Oxford and New York: B. Blackwell.

JEANS, SIR JAMES. Quoted in J. R. Newman (ed.) 1956. *The World of Mathematics.* New York: Simon and Schuster.

KAMII, C. 1985. *Young Children Reinvent Arithmetic.* New York: Teachers College Press.

KAMII, C. 1989. *Young Children Continue to Reinvent Arithmetic, Second Grade.* New York: Teachers College Press.

KAMII, C., and A. DOMINICK. 1998. "The harmful effects of algorithms in grades 1–4." In *The Teaching and Learning of Algorithms in School Mathematics,* eds. L. Morrow and M. Kenney. Reston, VA: National Council of Teachers of Mathematics.

KARLIN, S. 1983. Eleventh R. A. Fisher Memorial Lecture, Royal Society 20.

KELLOGG, R. 1969. *Analyzing Children's Art.* Palo Alto, CA: National Press Books.

KORTHAGEN, F., and J. KESSELS. 1999. "Linking Theory and Practice: Changing the Pedagogy of Teacher Education." *Educational Researcher* 28(4), 4–17.

LORENZ, J. H. 1997. "Is mental calculation just strolling around in an imaginary number space?" In *The Role of Contexts and Models in the Development of Mathematical Strategies and Procedures,* eds. M. Beishuizen, K. P. E. Gravemeijer, and E. C. D. M. van Lieshout. Utrecht: Utrecht University (CD-β series on research in education; 26), 199–213.

MA, L. 1999. *Knowing and Teaching Elementary Mathematics.* Mahwah, N.Y.: Erlbaum.

MCDUFF, D. 1991. *Mathematical Notices* 38(3), 185–7.

MORRIS, A. 1995. *Shoes, Shoes, Shoes.* New York: Lothrop Lee and Shepard.

NCTM, 2000. *Principles and Standards for School Mathematics.* Reston, VA: NCTM.

PASCAL, B. 1670. *Pensées de Pascal sur la religion et sur quelques autres subjets.* (n. ed.). Paris: Garnier.

PIAGET, J. 1965. *The Child's Conception of Number.* New York: Routledge.

PIAGET, J. 1977. *The Development of Thought: Equilibration of Cognitive Structures.* New York: Viking.

PLATO (ca. 429–347 B.C.). Quoted in J. R. Newman (ed.) 1956. *The World of Mathematics.* New York: Simon and Schuster.

POISSON, S. Quoted in *Mathematics Magazine* 64(1), 1991.

RESNICK, L., and S. F. OMANSON. 1987. "Learning to understand arithmetic." In *Advances in Instructional Psychology* 3, ed. R. Glaser. London: Lawrence Erlbaum.

SCHIFTER, D., and C. T. FOSNOT. 1993. *Reconstructing Mathematics Education Stories of Teachers Meeting the Challenge of Reform.* New York: Teachers College Press.

SIMON, M. 1995. "Reconstructing mathematics pedagogy from a constructivist perspective." *Journal for Research in Mathematics Education* 26, 114–45.

STREEFLAND, L. 1981. Cito's kommagetallen leerdoelgericht getoestst (1) [Cito's decimals tested in a criterion-referenced way (1)]. Willem Bartjens, 1 (1), 34–44. Cited in van den Heuvel-Panhuizen, M. (1996).

STREEFLAND, L. 1985. "Mathematics as an activity and reality as a source." *Niewe Wiskrant* 5(1), 60–67.

STREEFLAND, L. 1988. *Realistic Instruction of Fractions.* Utrecht: OW and OC, Utrecht University.

TERC. 1997, 1998. *Investigations in Space, Number, and Data.* Palo Alto, CA: Dale Seymour Publications.

TREFFERS, A. 1987. *Three dimensions. A model of goal and theory description in mathematics instruction—the Wiskobas Project.* Dordrecht: Reidel Publishing.

TREFFERS, A. 1991. "Realistic mathematics education in the Netherlands 1980–1990." In *Realistic Mathematics Education in Primary School,* ed. L. Streefland. Utrecht: Utrecht University (CD-β series on research in education; 9).

VAN DEN BRINK, F. J. 1991. "Realistic arithmetic education for young children." In *Realistic Mathematics Education in Primary School,* ed. L. Streefland. Utrecht: Utrecht University (CD-β series on research in education; 9).

VAN DEN HEUVEL-PANHUIZEN, M. 1996. *Assessment and Realistic Mathematic Education.* Utrecht: Utrecht University (CD-β series on research in education; 19).

VAN DEN HEUVEL-PANHUIZEN, M. 1999. Assessment for Mathematics in the City. Internal document. New York: City College of the City University of New York.

VAN DEN HEUVEL-PANHUIZEN, M. 2000. "Student Achievement in Mathematics in the City Viewed Through a Microscopic Lens." Paper presented at the International Conference of Mathematics Educators, Tokyo, Japan. August.

WEISBART, J. 2000. "Children's Notational Systems." Unpublished manuscript, City College of the City University of New York.

WEYL, H. Quoted in "Mathematics and the Laws of Nature." In *The Armchair Science Reader,* S. Sorkin and I. S. Gordon. 1959. New York: Simon and Schuster.

WHITENACK, J. W., N. KNIPPING, S. NOVINGER, and G. UNDERWOOD. In press. "Contexts for children's mathematical reasoning about tens and ones: The story of Aunt Mary's candies." *The Constructivist.*

WHITNEY, H. 1988. "Mathematical Reasoning, Early Grades." Unpublished manuscript, Princeton University, Princeton, NJ.

WYNN, K. 1998. "Psychological foundations of number: numerical competence in human infants." *Trends in Cognitive Sciences* 2, 296–303.

INDEX